No matter how prod
think you are, *How
Competition Into the Ground
and Have Fun Doing It*
can show you how to double
your output—and accomplish
more at work than you ever
imagined!

John T. Molloy's monumental best-seller *Dress for Success* forever changed the clothing styles of America's top corporate executives. Now his highly successful program for revolutionizing personal productivity among the nation's leading companies is available in book form for the first time.

Accessible, easy-to-follow, and effective, Molloy's step-by-step approach to changing the way you work can bring measurable results from the first day on! His proven techniques for analyzing individual weaknesses and strengths, time use, and overall output are personalized in this important book to fit your life-style and work demands. The result is a dramatic chance to change your competitive performance—and give yourself the winning edge today!

HOW TO WORK THE COMPETITION INTO THE GROUND AND HAVE FUN DOING IT

"Bound to become the bible on personal productivity. The executive suites in the '90's will undoubtedly be filled with the people Molloy has taught to work the competition into the ground."

—John Grady, President,
John Grady & Associates
formerly comptroller,
Booz, Allen & Hamilton, Inc.
and Peat, Marwick & Mitchell & Co.

Other books by John T. Molloy

Dress for Success*

The Woman's Dress for Success*

Live for Success

*published by Warner Books

—— John T. Molloy ——

HOW TO WORK THE COMPETITION INTO THE GROUND AND HAVE FUN DOING IT

A PROVEN PROGRAM TO RAISE YOUR PERSONAL PRODUCTIVITY

WARNER BOOKS

A Warner Communications Company

W A Warner Communications Company

Book Design by Nicola Mazzella
Printed in the United States of America
First Printing: January 1987
10 9 8 7 6 5 4 3 2 1

Library of Congress Cataloging-in-Publication Data

Molloy, John T.
  How to work the competition into the ground and have fun doing it.

  Includes index.
  1. Success in business. 2. Performance.   I. Title.
HF5386.M72 1987   650.1   86-24761
ISBN 0-446-38499-2 (U.S.A.) (p.b.k.)
0-446-38500-X (Canada) (p.b.k.)

To
Maureen and Robert,
who motivate my productivity.

Contents

INTRODUCTION

The Good News About Working

The good news is that after observing and interviewing several thousand of the most and least productive workers in more than sixty companies and running personal productivity courses for five years, I discovered several very exciting facts about working.

First, anyone can become a great worker. Great workers are not born, they're made. Almost every top worker I interviewed said that someone at some point in his life taught him how to work. That person helped him to develop a good set of work habits, and these habits have stuck with him and made him the good worker he is today. Which means if you're not a top performer, I can help you to become one.

Second, the personal productivity training course outlined in this book will enable you without great expense or extraordinary effort to increase your productivity if you follow a simple set of instructions. Almost everyone who has tried it, from the presidents of corporations, most of whom were wonderful workers, to people who were about to be fired because they weren't producing the minimum required by their bosses, became more effective workers. Naturally, different people will get different things from this book. Great workers will use this book the same way a great golfer would use a book on golf. They will look carefully with an expert's eye for hints that might give them that all-important edge they need when they are competing with other top performers, while the people who don't know how to work, like the neophyte golfer, will use this how-to book to learn the fundamentals.

Third, once you learn to work effectively, work becomes fun. When I first interviewed top workers, they told me how hard they worked, how often they burnt the midnight oil, how many days they spent away from home, and all the other sacrifices they made. These very dedicated workers assumed that working hard meant suffering, so they told me how much they suffered. I almost believed them until I started questioning them about their jobs and about the things they've accomplished. Then their tone changed. The facts remained the same but the message was different. Those very effective workers all of a sudden started to sound like marathon runners. They still talked about sweat and sacrifice, but now they did it with the pride of one who has fought the good fight and won. They worked for money and position, and they enjoyed the rewards in the same way marathon runners enjoyed cheers and trophies, but the real reason they put forth extraordinary effort is they're competing with themselves, and when they win in that competition they believe a better person emerges. Like marathon runners, they experience an emotional high when theoretically they're suffering the most. And because they have a heck of a lot of fun outperforming the competition, they do it all the time—and you can as well.

Fourth, the real secret of success is no secret at all: it is effective work. Over 95 percent of the twenty thousand successful men and women we've interviewed over the past twenty-five years agree that if you set realistic goals for yourself and work hard to achieve them, you will almost invariably succeed. Success, money, power, and achievement go to those who know how to work.

Fifth, creativity is not a gift of the gods but a teachable skill. My interviews with creative people uncovered the fact that creativity depends on method, not madness, and by copying the methods of creative people you are much more likely to be creative.

I also discovered that productive people are not only more likely to be rich, successful, and creative but happy as well. If you want you, your children, or your employees to lead happier and more productive lives, read on.

CHAPTER ONE

The History of Jobnastics

How I Started

During my last year in college I was not very happy. It was at that point I realized that a degree in Liberal Arts was almost worthless in the job market and decided I would have to acquire some type of technical training, either by joining a firm that offered technical training or by continuing my education.

It was for that reason that I turned down an offer to join an executive training program in a large manufacturing corporation and took a job with an insurance company that included technical training. Unfortunately, the job didn't provide real technical training or a real challenge. It was too easy. After two months of boredom I took an extra job at night, worked in my spare time as a freelance reporter, and attempted to write a book. I didn't realize at the time that I had to do all those things, but I understand now that the school system which gave me two or three hours of homework in grade school, more in high school and more in college had not only taught me to work but made work an essential part of my life.

In 1961 I left the insurance company, and went to work as a teacher. When I started I was shocked by the deterioration of the school system since I had graduated, and in the eight years I taught, the deterioration accelerated. By the time I left, most of the young people graduating from high school were incapable of performing work at any level. I realized that the educational system was turning out young people who could not work. What I didn't realize was the terrible effect it was having on me.

A Personal Productivity Problem

When I first started working as a full-time image consultant, I had a very simple procedure. I gave lectures on wardrobe engineering to large groups, and then conducted individual sessions with top executives or with key people in the company. I had each client bring a half dozen outfits to these sessions, and, using these outfits, I did an analysis of their business wardrobes and gave them specific suggestions on how to improve them. After conducting these sessions for six or seven months, I found myself inundated with clients and buried with work. All of a sudden these executives numbered in the thousands, and they were sending me swatches of material from all over the country and asking me to pick shirts and ties to match their new suits. As a result, I spent much of my time running up and down Fifth Avenue buying shirts and ties instead of consulting.

I finally reached the point that it became physically impossible for me to carry on any longer. I was about to sit down and write to my clients and tell them that I couldn't supply them with clothing anymore, when suddenly, I had what I still think was a brilliant idea. I opened a small shirt and tie store and stocked it with all of the items I needed to supply my clients. The number of orders that I had for shirts and ties from around the country paid the rent without my having to worry about a walk-in clientele. In addition, the business gave me a credit rating which enabled me to produce and sell uniforms (still one of my largest businesses).

Although the store was one of the best business ideas I ever had, it almost ruined me. It was a small operation and it didn't have an entrance on the street, which limited the number of walk-in customers. Actually that was part of its appeal. I had the store divided into two areas: a front section to deal with customers, and a back room that doubled as storage space and a research office. When I opened, my plan was to hire a clerk, and to spend most of my time in the office working on research. After a month or two, I realized that wasn't happening. Although the store was doing fine, I hadn't completed two days of research in all that time. When I analyzed what was going wrong, I found to my surprise that I had been looking out the window, listening to the radio, and doing what my grandmother called lollygagging. Like most people who find they aren't doing what they're supposed to be doing, I made excuses for myself. I told myself that I was just starting in business and it was all new to me. I had to get into it, and now that I was used to it I'd get back to work. I was determined to turn over a new leaf and believed that the simple act of will was all that was necessary for me to start being productive once again. To my shock, chagrin, and surprise, I found I *couldn't* work. No matter how much effort I put into my work, I didn't produce nearly as much as I thought I should. It wasn't because I didn't try. I gave it everything I had, but somehow that just wasn't enough. Finally, after about three months, on a slow, rainy Friday afternoon in February, I found myself sitting looking out a window, in spite of my decision earlier that day to work. I realized that I really had tried to work that day but somehow I couldn't. Which meant that I had lost my ability to work, and, if I were to regain it again, I'd have to retrain myself.

Retraining Myself to Work

The moment I came to this decision I should have acted. However, the idea that I had to retrain myself to work annoyed me. It struck me as being unfair. I held the belief for years that knowing how to work is like riding a bicycle: once you knew how you never forgot. I tried to hang on to that belief in spite of the facts. But I couldn't; and, once I faced the reality that I needed real help, I developed a plan. I decided that the only logical method would be to calculate exactly how much work I was doing. I attempted to recreate the jobs I had finished during the last several months, so that I could measure what I had actually accomplished against what I should have accomplished. I discovered I was producing even less than I'd originally thought. When I asked myself why, the answer was simple. I had trouble concentrating. Concentration, which had come to me so naturally in the past, now eluded me. Where at one time I had the ability to sit for hours and work without interruption, my mind now flew out the window, with or without my permission, with annoying regularity.

I decided that my years as a teacher had robbed me of my ability to work. Although I worked long hours as a teacher correcting compositions, I never worked under pressure. I corrected papers and did lesson plans at my own speed. The graduate courses I took as a teacher were snaps. I used to call them tail-callus courses. All you had to do was sit in one place and develop calluses on your tail, and you got a grade. They were ludicrously easy. Even the courses in subject matter were simple. The classes were generally loaded with teachers and geared to them. I know it's going to come as a shock to some, but most of the graduate courses given in teachers' colleges are watered down by professors who are convinced that teachers aren't ready, willing, or able to do first-class work. In such an environment it is no wonder I became mentally flabby.

Realizing this should have been very disheartening; but it wasn't, because the minute I started measuring my work I found that I automatically increased my productivity. I didn't know exactly how much I was improving, but I knew that the old form was coming back and that sooner or later I'd be back in the groove. I was convinced that buried under all those layers of mental fat was the good old John T. Molloy who could work twelve to sixteen hours a day and party afterwards. I knew I still had the energy and the ability to perform at a high level, and that if I got myself in shape I'd be able to do so once again.

Searching for a Better Method

Being a good researcher, I applied research techniques to my own rehabilitation. I tried to be as analytical as possible, and attempted to look at my problem from the perspective of a third party. After several false starts, I divided my work into a series of small digestible and measurable units, and then I attempted to estimate the best time at which I'd be able to undertake each unit. What I actually did was to sit down and estimate how long it would take good old hard-working, effective John T. Molloy to do the job, and set out to match that time. On the first couple of jobs I didn't do well because I was guessing at the amount of time I spent on a job. But I corrected that very quickly. I ran out and bought a stopwatch, which is the first thing I tell anyone to do who is trying to improve his productivity.

After measuring my work with a stopwatch, I found that I was working at about 62 percent of my potential, even after the improvement caused by measurement. The first thing I did was decide to immediately become the good old John T. Molloy, and I charged at my work. I put my head down and worked as hard as I could. And on the first few small jobs it looked as if I was going to make it, but the fact is the faster I ran, the less distance I covered. So once again, I stepped back and attempted to analyze my problem as if I were a third party. From that perspective, I could see that a decision to increase my performance on a regular but measured basis of approximately 10 percent a week made a lot more sense than attempting to correct everything overnight.

Because I'd been a good worker, it was easy for me to teach myself to be one again. There's a series of reasons for it, but the most important one is that once you develop a physical or mental skill, even if you lose that skill through lack of practice, you can reacquire it more quickly than someone who's never had it. Your nervous system remembers, even if you don't. If you're a golfer, you know the feel of a good swing. If you're a dancer, you'll know when you start moving with the music. And if you're a worker, you'll know when you're working again. Once you start rolling, things will come easily to you. Therefore, if you're my age and you've been taught to work and you've been a great worker, once you start training yourself there will be a dramatic increase in your productivity. However, you can't expect that type of improvement from the young people who have never learned to work. It's going to take them a bit longer.

I must tell you my improvement didn't take place overnight. No one's ever does—it takes work. In fact, it took me close to a year to get back into "working shape." I was working at my potential long before that, but at the end of the year I was doing it without enormous effort. I used a very simple method to train myself. Having already measured my productivity in several critical areas, I set up a reward and punishment system to encourage myself to work harder. Every time I outperformed my last effort or exceeded my personal goal, I rewarded myself. For about four months I did so by feeding myself the most delicious Italian chocolate creams in the world. When I worked below my last performance, I punished myself, in the beginning, by working a half hour extra on the job; but I soon gave that up because work was no longer a punishment. I instead gave up lunch any time I didn't perform well. And by that time giving up lunch was a great idea, because those wonderful, delicious Italian chocolate creams had put about ten pounds on me.

Up to this point it was all hard work—all sweat, all toil. Although the end product had a certain degree of satisfaction built into it, I wasn't getting tremendous satisfaction out of my work. But then all of a sudden I broke the barrier, both the pain barrier and the work barrier. I started to outperform even the old John T. Molloy. But I only did that after I made a discovery that one never performs beyond one's expectation. We all have four-minute miles in our lives, and we must remove those psychological barriers if we are to increase our performance.

Changing Expectations

I realized that I had to change my expectation of performance after I had lunch with a former student who is now an attorney. He had been a member of one of the debating teams I coached. That team was particularly talented and hard working, and they ran over every other high school in the area. I was preparing them for a state championship, but there was no one in the immediate vicinity who was capable of keeping them on their toes. So I went to a local university and asked the debating coach if he would allow his college debaters to debate my high-school students. He pointed out that they were debating a different topic, but said if my students were willing to prepare that year's college topic he would be glad to take them on. He also pointed out that his team were state champions and that my people wouldn't do very well against them.

After the first debate we knew he was right: our team didn't do well at all. Those college youngsters were terrific, and my debaters came home dejected and beaten. The next day we discussed what mistakes they'd made; and we asked for a second debate, and then a third, and then a fourth, and then a fifth, and each time they learned a bit more, and each time they left they were a little bit less dejected and a little bit less beaten. Although they never won or even came close to winning when debating this excellent college team, they went on to become the high-school state champions. In fact, they ran away with it. They were head and shoulders above their high-school competition, because their expectations of what was necessary to be good debaters had risen dramatically as a result of competing with a top-notch college team.

After lunching with my former student, I had an idea. I immediately went to a chart I had on my wall and changed it. In the original chart I was measuring everything against the good old John T. Molloy who was at the top of the chart. What I did was take down that chart and put up a new one, and on this chart the good old John T. Molloy was in the middle, and at the top of the chart was super John T. Molloy—the person who could and would outwork everyone in the world. Once I did that my productivity increased dramatically. Expectation is a critical factor and you must expect yourself not to be merely as good as you can be, but better than you can be.

My First Students

Two years later I'd forgotten my problem. Work by that time was once again as natural to me as breathing, when I had a young man thrust upon me by a client company. I had agreed to take one of their employees, and train him to be an in-house image consultant. The employee was to work for me for three months familiarizing himself with our research and consulting procedures, and then return to his company and, under my direction, put those procedures to work.

When the young man arrived the first day I gave him an assignment, and at the end of the day I was very angry when I discovered he hadn't half finished it. I told him I wasn't happy with his performance and I expected him to work more efficiently the next day, and I gave him an additional assignment so that he would have something to do when he finished the first one. On the following day I was unexpectedly called out of the office and didn't get back for over a week. When I returned I found that the young man hadn't made any substantial progress on either assignment. I called him into my office, sat him down, and told him I wasn't going to put up with that type of nonsense. I told him that his company expected me to produce a certain amount of work and to use him to do it, and that if he wasn't going to take his job seriously, I was going to go back to his boss and ask for a replacement. I told him I assumed he knew that such a request would probably have a very negative impact on his career, and I didn't want to do that, so I was going to give him one last chance. I told him that when he came to work the next day, he'd better work—or else.

I was very annoyed with him, but I softened a little when he admitted he was goofing off and promised to buckle down and improve. He went on to explain that he had been out of the army for only two weeks and that he'd got into awful habits while in the service. He'd been the only college graduate in a typing pool and apparently the only one who could spell and punctuate. Most of the others, including the sergeant, were high-school dropouts who got their diplomas in the army; so he was the shining star without doing any work. He was the best typist and invariably was assigned to do work for the colonel for an hour and a half to two hours a day, and the rest of the time he sat around and did nothing. He assured me that that was over now and he would get down to work on Monday.

The next week he was trying. He sat down and pushed himself. But although I could see the intense effort on his face, I could also see he wasn't accomplishing too much. By Tuesday afternoon I decided that he had to make some definite improvements or I'd have to get rid of him. Once again I called him into my office and spoke to him. This time he insisted that he was really trying, but said he simply couldn't concentrate. His mind kept jumping out the window. He was as surprised as I had been two years earlier that he couldn't concentrate. He went on to tell me he had been a good student in school, and all of a sudden I recognized his problem—it's the problem I'd had two years earlier. The army had done the same thing to him that teaching had done to me. It had turned his work muscle into a flabby mess. But I doubted, even as he was talking to me, that he had ever been a first-class worker.

I explained to him that I at least partially understood his problem, and I told him that if he was willing to work overtime at his own cost to help solve the problem, I would train him to work. I promised that I would hold off asking for a replacement until I'd seen how he did. Frankly, a consultant never wants to go back to a company and say, "You sent me a lousy employee." It doesn't do the consultant any more good than it does the employee.

Once I committed myself to training him, I found I had taken on more work than I really wanted. When I trained myself I did all sorts of mental record keeping. But once I started working with this young man, I realized I had to keep written records, and the procedure was very time consuming. If I hadn't already committed myself, I probably would have forgotten the whole thing.

I followed the same procedures with him as I did with myself. I broke his work down into digestible bits that could be measured, not only by him but by me. I then set him to work measuring his actual production against what we both agreed should be his ideal production. Once we determined that he was working at about 60 percent of his potential, we set a goal of increasing his productivity by 20 percent a week. Unfortunately that goal was unrealistic and we had to adjust it. Once we did adjust the goal downwards, he moved ahead at a smooth, measured pace, making small but sure gains. I used the same methods to increase his work skills as I'd used to increase my own. A little bit at a time. A little strain, a little pain, a little gain. Never too much, and always redoing and rechecking.

His training turned out to be an excellent management tool, and it served both my interest and his. As it happened, the young man was very conscientious and he worked very hard at improving not only his work skills but his production. At the end of three months he was working as well as any young person I had ever hired, and doing a very creditable job. Unfortunately, he didn't stay with the company that sent him. He chose to go to law school; I lost him as an in-house consultant and had to retrain his replacement, who unfortunately had no better work habits than he. The only difference was that my new trainee was a female. When she arrived I immediately recognized that there was little difference between her productivity and his. Rather than waste my time with her, I sat her down immediately, identified the problem, and told her what we were going to do about it if she wished to remain in my employ. The young woman improved at even a more rapid rate than her predecessor. Her production increased by geometric leaps. Within three or four weeks she was performing at a very high level. I was so happy with the results of her training that I started training all of the young people who came to work for me.

The people assigned to me as consultants unfortunately needed the training. They weren't even college students of average ability, they were often productivity basket cases. The companies I worked for certainly didn't send me their best people. I discovered that most young people coming to me had very little sense of organization, and hardly any good work habits. They needed a set of specific instructions on how to perform the technical aspects of the job, how to organize it and how to control it; and they needed someone to sit over them and help them measure their productivity and to insist that they increase it. I did this because they were spending my money.

Why I Call It Jobnastics

About a year later I had a young man come to work for me who was a jock at New York University. I don't know in which sports he participated. It was through my association with him that I coined the term jobnastics. He was the one who first started using athletic terms to describe what we were doing. He kept talking about getting himself into mental shape, wearing off his mental fat, trimming down for a particular job, and revving up to get to it. I found myself acting as his coach. He was a pleasant and likable young man, a natural leader among the three I was training; and he tried to take over the training. It was because he was so competitive that I went along with using his sports jargon and adopted it, at first almost in a kidding manner. Then I realized the validity of what he was saying. I suddenly saw that there were great similarities in training people for specific athletic activities and for specific jobs.

While almost everyone involved in any physical activity can improve his performance by physical conditioning, the type of exercise an athlete would undertake would depend on the sport in which he was to participate. A football lineman would spend more time developing his strength by lifting weights than a long-distance runner would. Although the runner might lift weights, it wouldn't be a primary exercise. He would probably spend his time exercising his cardiovascular system and increasing his lung power. The general statement that both would be better athletes if they were in better condition would be true, but conditioning for each means something different.

I found the same principle applied when I was training researchers. The researchers who were doing field work had a double function: they were administrators who had to supervise the young men and women who were in the field talking to people; at the same time they had to monitor the responses, because if anything unusual started to affect the direction of the research, we would want to know right away. Instant accurate analysis of data by field supervisors could save thousands of dollars, and sometimes an entire research project. Therefore, the people holding those positions had to be able to analyze statistical data very rapidly. The people doing statistical analysis back in the office required a different set of skills. Quick analysis was not required; what was required was attention to detail.

So the type of training I gave each one varied, although the basic techniques remained the same. A coach analyzes what an athlete has to do and then tailors his training to his needs and his sport; a work coach has to do the same thing.

Clients Wanted Training

Up to this point all of the information I'd gathered on productivity was designed totally for in-house use. I was using it to make my people effective, and had no intention of training anyone outside my company. But since many of the people who worked for me were borrowed from client companies, I ended up training people who worked for Fortune 500 companies. In a number of cases, when those people returned to their companies, they were far more effective workers in the eyes of their superiors than when they'd left. Executives in several firms became interested in why the change took place and asked their employees. When they found out this change took place as a result of my training, they showed great interest.

One company in particular was very interested in my methods and asked me to help them set up personal productivity courses in-house. I explained that a tremendous amount of time and effort was needed to conduct these courses, and that I simply didn't have the time. But I agreed to make up a little training manual so that their management personnel could take the course themselves and give it to their employees.

About two and a half years later, I was contacted by the company and asked if I would sign away my rights to the productivity training system that I had developed. What they wanted was the right to print unlimited numbers of my pamphlet. I initially said no because although I had been refining the technique for two and a half years, the pamphlet was still a crude document. However, they believed that I was negotiating and what they did was sweeten the pot. They offered me a rather substantial figure if I would sign over all rights to my system, including the right to say that I had developed it. Naturally I said no, and I decided that if they were that interested, possibly other corporate clients would be also. After making a few phone calls, I decided to write this book. I believed I could do it in three or four months. It's taken three years because I wanted to be able to say to the reader, not "I think you can increase your personal productivity if you follow the instructions in this book," but "I'm sure you can"—and I am. Read on. This book can make you a better, more successful worker, and, as a result, a happy worker—and, since most of us spend most of our waking hours at work or engaging in work, a happy person.

CHAPTER TWO

Motivation

The IBM Song Book

After having given a presentation to a group of engineers in southern California, I asked if anyone at the table knew of an antiquarian book store. I collect first editions, and when I have a couple of hours to kill before a plane I go looking for old books. Although no one at the table knew where one was located, someone did ask me which book I would most like to own, and I told him that I would like to own the IBM song book. I said that I'd heard of it, but I'd never seen one. The minute I finished that sentence, an IBM manager sitting at the table cleared his throat. He looked obviously upset. He said that he had worked for IBM for ten years and he'd never seen a song book, and he'd never met anyone who had seen a song book. He thought it was a myth put out by IBM competitors to make IBM look stodgy and out-of-date. He went on to say that IBM wasn't old-fashioned and out-of-date, and it didn't require things of its employees that other companies didn't. The whole idea of a song book seemed ridiculous to him; he assumed that the reason I'd never seen it was that it probably never existed. Not wanting to argue with him, I agreed that the stories I'd heard were probably apocryphal, apologized for bringing up the subject, and decided not to bring it up again, especially in the company of IBMers.

Japanese Motivation

That night I caught the red-eye to New York because I had a meeting with the president of a large Japanese company at the New York Hilton the next morning. I had already signed a contract with that company to design their uniform, and one of the conditions in the contract was that I meet with the president. I assumed that the purpose of the meeting was simply to let him eyeball me so that he could feel comfortable with the man who was going to impact his company in a major way, but I was mistaken. When I showed up the following morning expecting just a polite breakfast meeting, I found the room filled with cameras, projectors, and assistants. He immediately went to work. He started by talking about his company. He said that I had to understand the nature of his company before I could design a uniform that was suitable. He told me that his company was a family, a true family, and they cared for one another, and everyone contributed his best to the family, and naturally they were all interested in the family doing as well as possible. He went on to explain that it was his job, as head of the company, to lead the family. He wanted a uniform that sent this family message.

He showed me films of a number of company meetings, and translated and explained what was going on in the film clips. The films were all really the same. They showed cheering sessions for the company. There was one film showing the line people attending a pep rally before starting work on a new product. It was as close to an American high-school pep rally as anything I've ever witnessed, and I've never seen its equivalent in American industry. He also showed me how his employees started each morning, with exercises and the company chant. The entire point of the film clips and the meeting was to stress the importance of this esprit de corps in the company. He wanted me to know that his employees had a feeling akin to patriotism for the company, and that that was the feeling that the uniform I was designing must help foster.

I couldn't help contrasting this Japanese executive and his American counterpart. While the executive at IBM thought I was making fun of his company when I mentioned a company song book, his Japanese counterpart bragged about having a company chant. I'm sure if this Japanese gentleman's company had a song, he would have sung it for me, because he thought that it was his job as president of the company to spend three hours with the man who was going to design his uniform so that I would understand the feelings that his employees had for this company, and how these feelings helped motivate them and make his company profitable. He was proud of his company's cheer, not ashamed of it, not embarrassed by it, because he believed it was critical to his company's success. His IBM counterpart thought that as a sophisticated executive he must deny the existence of such sentimentality and parochialism in his company, while the Japanese executive thought that being sophisticated required that he recognize these qualities. Halfway through the presentation, I understood exactly what he was after, and I became a bit depressed. I saw that American companies, including our most effective ones, which certainly includes IBM, were going to find it very difficult to compete with this unashamed gentleman and his corny, sentimental, song-singing, but highly motivated, workers.

American Industries Must Motivate

There are several steps that American industry must take if they wish to compete with these very highly motivated Japanese companies. First, there should be regular motivational sessions for all employees, not just the salespeople. A company should send its best line worker as well as the best salesperson to Hawaii, and of course there has to be a system that rewards productivity. Any American company that can put in bonus systems similar to those of the Japanese companies will do very well. In Japan a substantial percentage of most employees' income depends on how well their companies have done. This gives them a tremendous incentive to be productive, and their attitude toward their work is much different from ours. You will never see a Japanese employee let a bad product go past him on a line simply because the mistake isn't his personal responsibility. He believes that he's responsible for the entire company and its productivity. Several American companies have instituted similar programs with a great deal of success.

Managers must also stop thinking that management decisions alone can make the average worker more productive. Our interviews with productive and unproductive workers indicate that managers have much less effect than they think. People are more productive when they're taught to work and are rewarded for working. In fact, you can only teach them to work if they are motivated and rewarded for working. Otherwise they will ignore the teaching.

I deal with American executives all the time. They're not only customers, but they're my friends and my buddies, so I get feedback on my ideas from them; and when I read this section to many of them, their instant reaction was, "What a terrific idea, our people should be cheering too."

Unfortunately, their next reaction was, "Let's see now, who in my company can do it? I think I'll get Charlie, the vice president of personnel, and put him in charge of cheering. That sounds good." The fact is, as soon as Charlie gets the order, he passes it down to someone else. As a result, the cheering is led by someone who's only a couple of steps above the person who's supposed to cheer. Consequently, the person doing the cheerleading is not the best one to be doing it. In fact, in most companies the vice president in charge of human resources is not the best person to be doing the cheerleading. Our research indicates that the CEO is the only person to be doing the cheerleading, and should be the company's top cheerleader. If he is to be effective in this role, he must be seen not only cheering, but working. Both he and the other top executives must be seen by their employees rolling up their sleeves and going to work. These executives should be living examples of hard work. They must be as dedicated to their company as they expect their employees to be, because when they're not, they're not kidding anyone.

Unfortunately, in America today there are not many dedicated executives. A number of those I know personally at or near the top of American corporations have very little loyalty to their companies. They look upon them as trading partners. They trade their services for a certain amount of money, power, and benefits, and that's the end of it. As a result, they don't give their best to the companies. Their relationship is impersonal at best, and sometimes antagonistic. The reason for this unhealthy relationship is not the fault of the individual executive; it's the fault of a system that has developed over a period of years. Management decisions, made mainly by M.B.A.-trained executives, say that the immediate bottom line is all that counts; and, in the name of immediate profits, they encourage top executives to hop from one company to another in much the same way Hollywood starlets supposedly hop from bed to bed. As a result, executives' relationships with their companies are intense, but short in duration and meaningless. If America is going to produce a highly motivated work force, it has to have a highly motivated executive corps, composed of executives who, even if they don't spend a lifetime with the company, expect that they might. If the way up is always the way out, you're never going to have anyone giving their all for a company. They will give whatever they think they need to give to get by.

Our best and most successful companies are companies that have a very small turnover among their executives. They're companies that promote from within. They're companies that reward productivity. They're companies that expect loyalty and dedication from all of their employees, both white collar and blue collar, and return it to them. They're companies that are respected by their employees, and that respect their employees.

A Finishing School for Executives

The most successful program my company runs I've dubbed "a finishing school for executives." We teach executives, would-be executives, and those who want to or have to deal with executives, how to dress, walk, talk, shake hands, sit, stand, and eat like executives. We spend from four hours to four days giving this course, and the individuals who take it spend from four weeks to a year practicing those visual and verbal signals that will make them more persuasive and more powerful. The course is so popular that I can no longer keep up with the requests to conduct it. As a result, I'm now preparing to put it on satellites, so that instead of teaching hundreds, I can teach thousands at one sitting.

However, I must tell you that it's not the course that I would like to give. I would like to give the Japanese equivalent of my course. Theirs isn't a finishing school for executives, theirs is a West Point for executives. When young men and women enter West Point, they spend time in "Beast Barracks." During that time they are pushed and driven almost past the point of endurance. Young Japanese executives have almost an identical training. They are taken away for several weeks, put in uniforms, and driven for seventeen hours a day. Technically, they're being taught the same thing American executives are being taught in my course—the social graces of business. While we teach people to shake hands, they spend hours teaching people to bow. While we teach executives how to be more authoritative by dropping their voices and changing their body posture, the Japanese teach their executives to be more authoritative by being louder and more piercing.

The objective of the training is the same; however, there are two major differences. First, the Japanese training is done under pressure, similar to a West Pointer's. West Point assumes that their people are going to have to act under pressure during their careers. The Japanese assume that there is as much pressure in industry as there is in combat, and they train their people to participate in industrial war. I think they're correct in that assumption. Next, when I give the course, no one fails. As a result, no one really succeeds. In the Japanese course one-fourth to one-third of the participants fail. They know before they enter that a percentage of these bright, talented, articulate, and upwardly mobile people aren't going to make it, and it's going to have a devastating effect on their careers; so the pressure is enormous, and the sense of accomplishment when they succeed is as well. The Japanese do let some of their best and brightest people take the course a second time, but others are simply washed out of the fast track. It is this pressure training that gives the Japanese an office corps suitable for their industrial marine corps, while we have an office corps suitable for our industrial national guard.

I do not believe that the Japanese mentality or training should or could be transplanted in America. I do not believe that American corporations should send their executives away for weeks to be trained to use the proper fork. The formalities are not as important in this society as they are in Japan. However, I do believe that the American training, although shorter in duration, should be just as severe, just as trying, just as testing—and I also believe it will not take place. It will not take place because American executives in their misplaced self-confidence are not ready to take that step. And because they're not, American corporations won't supply the support system that the Japanese do for the well-motivated worker—at least not in the foreseeable future.

Which means whether you're an American executive, a blue-collar worker, or self-employed, you're going to have to help yourself, because no one else is going to help you. Although it sounds very difficult, it really isn't as difficult as it seems. I haven't come up with a substitute for will-power, which would make it easy, but I've come up with the next best thing.

Six months after I started training myself to work, I sat back and analyzed my progress, and decided that although I had dramatically increased my productivity, I was not working near my capacity. I was working effectively by almost any measurement in American society today, but I knew I could do a lot more, and could do it better. My problem wasn't that I didn't want to do it better. You've never met anyone who, at least on the surface, seemed to be trying any harder. My problem was sustaining my motivation. I would push myself to what I considered my limit, and produce as much as possible for a day, sometimes even a week, but sooner or later I'd slip. I couldn't maintain maximum effort over a long period of time.

I had developed all sorts of devices to help myself be more productive. One of the most successful was a slogan a day. Every night before I went to bed, I picked a slogan, wrote it out, and pasted it on my bathroom mirror. In the beginning my slogans were general: *I will work harder. I will produce more. I will concentrate.* But after a short period of time, they became more specific, and more effective. I started saying: *I will finish the Jones job in two hours. I will not leave my desk until the Smith job is perfect. I will not be satisfied with anything less than finishing a particular research project on a particular day.* And I found myself working very effectively on those projects I singled out for this type of attention. However, at best, this produced sporadic high productivity, not consistent peak performance. I also found that on certain mornings I would forget to set a goal for the day. And what was worse, there was a tremendous temptation to backslide. My gains in productivity, although real, had not become part of my personality. I was not naturally a productive worker. I was still a poor worker forcing himself to be productive. And when I realized that I hadn't gone back to being the enormously productive John T. Molloy, I became a little discouraged and decided to take a week off from my productivity training.

Meeting an Old Student

During that week I made several trips out of the city, and while walking through La Guardia Airport I met an ex-student of mine. This student, whose name I won't use, was living proof that Father Flanagan was wrong when he said there was no such thing as a bad boy. He was disruptive, lazy, a liar, insulting to his teachers and his parents —a youngster with some natural ability who only used his intelligence to create disruption. He was disliked by the teachers, by the other students, and I suspect by his parents. In all my years of teaching, I never met anyone else who caused so much trouble for so many people, and did it so consistently. You couldn't get him to go along with anything. If everyone wanted chocolate ice cream, he would put his body on the railroad track to get vanilla. If everyone wanted vanilla, he would go to the track for chocolate. In spite of all the trouble he caused, I had a grudging admiration for him. He was totally independent. He displayed a perverse type of courage. He stood up under pressure from his parents, his peers, his teachers on numerous occasions, and always successfully. That's why I was shocked to see him in the middle of La Guardia Airport, dressed like a fugitive from Shangri-La, with a blank look on his face, selling flowers. This young man, whose only positive attribute was his independence, was willingly peddling flowers so that some little self-appointed messiah could live in palaces and drive Rolls-Royces while he dressed in clothing inadequate to keep him warm on that bitter January day.

Naturally, I stopped, and, although he recognized me, all he did was parrot the party line, "Buy a flower and save the world." I bought one in hopes of getting him to talk to me, not out of any desire to save him from the life he had chosen, but to satisfy my curiosity. Why was he there? To me it was a total mystery. If I'd picked one student who wouldn't be conned by such an obvious fraud, it would have been him. I couldn't get him to talk to me. He just kept parroting the party line—contribute more money to my wonderful leader and save the world—so I left.

Brainwashing Yourself

The next day on my way back to New York, I was engrossed by an article in one of the news magazines. It was about the deprogramming controversy, and it contained detailed descriptions of how fringe groups capture young people as well as the efforts of their parents to get them back. The article described the programming techniques used by these cults—how they deprived young people of sleep and protein, and used a technique called "love bombing" to psychologically trap them. The article was interesting on its own merit, but it absolutely fascinated me because I'd met the boy in the airport just the day before. After we landed I once again retraced my steps through the airport and saw this pathetic young man standing in the same place. A light went on. I wondered if I could brainwash myself to be more effective, using the techniques used by these fringe groups, but for a positive rather than negative purpose.

The minute I had the thought, the thought repelled me. My reaction to brainwashing was just about the same as everyone else's. It's one of those terms that immediately sets up a psychological red flag. The minute most of us hear it, we become annoyed, or at least defensive. In our mind's eye, we see prisoners in hovels being psychologically and physically tortured. Or we see the end products of these fringe groups, once promising young people now with blank expressions on their faces, performing a variety of mindless tasks. The whole idea has an element of terror built into it, but if you think about it for just a few minutes, you'll see that the techniques themselves are not necessarily evil. What is evil is the way they are being used. Controlling your mind can be a very positive step if you do it for a positive purpose. Once I came to this conclusion, I decided to look carefully at the techniques the cults used and see if I could apply some of them to improve my training as a worker.

The Motivators

The first thing I found is that these fringe groups will do anything to get young people to go away with them for a weekend. They want to take potential converts away from their normal environment, isolate them, and surround them with only members of the cult. And although this technique has no real application for individuals, it's terrific if you're working with half a dozen people who are willing to spend some time with one another in a self-help group. Instead of "Love Bombing," we call it "Confidence Building." Two groups, one a group of attorneys and the second a group of engineers, tried it for a weekend and found it very effective. They all were working on the same project, and instead of working in their normal office environment, they took their project to an isolated area. The lawyers chose a resort, the engineers went to a house owned by one of them in the mountains. They took their papers and the paraphernalia they needed, and they worked together and they worked around the clock. While each one attempted to measure his own productivity, they encouraged and helped one another with such admonitions as "You can do it," "You're terrific," "You're a valued member of the best team in the world," etc. They referred to it as work bombing rather than love bombing, and both groups said that their projects went beautifully, and that individuals felt more productive when they finished. In fact, both groups now have regularly scheduled work retreats. Anytime they're going to be dealing with a major project, they attempt to set up an isolated work environment in which they attack the project as a team. The projects invariably get the very best the team is capable of, and the individuals come out refreshed and in shape to work.

The article in the news magazine reported that these religious charlatans kept young people awake for long hours, and put them under psychological as well as physical pressure, because under such conditions they were susceptible to suggestion. Up to this point in my training, when I awoke every morning I repeated a series of positive phrases with the hopes of giving myself a positive mind-set for that day. All of a sudden I realized that I was attacking my mind when it was freshest. I was trying to indoctrinate myself at the wrong time. Obviously, if the experts at brain-washing first exhausted their subjects, it seemed logical that I would be best able to program myself at the end of the day, particularly at the end of a long day.

Motivational Tapes

With this in mind, I arranged my schedule so that two weeks later I was working sixteen to twenty hours a day. At the end of these very long days I played a tape that I had recorded with a series of positive messages. I lay in bed and listened to the messages and attempted to repeat them. This is the only change I made in my programming. On Friday of that week, I went up to my place in the country, brought my tapes with me, and continued to work at this breakneck pace. Only now the conditioning went on full-time. As I worked, ate, slept, I played the tapes over and over. I kept the volume so that the messages were audible but not disturbing. I called them the elevator music of success. I restated that I will be better organized in fifteen different ways, and I sent myself that message at least every half hour, along with a series of other messages. At the end of the weekend, I returned to the city and gave myself a well-deserved day off. When I returned to work Tuesday, it was immediately evident that the weekend of self-indoctrination or brainwashing had had an enormous effect upon my ability to work. For the next two weeks, almost without effort, I worked at top speed with optimum results. I very seldom let my mind drift, and had almost complete control over my emotions. I was back to being the old productive John T. Molloy. However, at the end of the second week I started to slip; so I began to make great effort once again to maintain focus for long periods of time.

When I thought about it, the reason was obvious. I had indoctrinated myself for a week and then stopped, while the experts in the cults had ongoing programs. I decided I needed an ongoing program as well and started playing the tapes every night. I made those tapes an essential part of my life, and played them over and over before I went to bed. In less than a week I had once more become an effective worker. Once again I'd become a natural, and could work at top speed without tremendous effort. Once I'd begun playing the tapes regularly I started to experiment. One night I filled my bathtub with warm water, put a rubber pillow behind my head, lay back, and played the tapes. I found that the tapes seemed to be more effective in that setting. I'm not sure why this worked, but I'm sure that it did work better. This method was so comfortable and relaxing that, in addition to being more effective, it solved the main problem I had with programming myself at night. I often became so excited about what I was going to do the next day that I had trouble sleeping. By playing the tapes like background music at a barely audible level, I relaxed myself, and when I did this sitting in a warm bathtub, in a comfortable chair, or lying in bed with my eyes closed, it helped me sleep. This became my favorite method. Although I have no statistical evidence that it works better than any other method, hundreds of people who have gone through the program absolutely swear by it and have sent in report after report about the miracles it has worked for them.

I must put in a word of warning at this point. We had one young man who almost drowned in the bathtub, because he was on medication when he tried this. Don't attempt this procedure if you are taking medication or if you're drinking. It could be very dangerous. Equally dangerous could be undertaking any of the procedures in the book which require that you put yourself under stress without the advice of a doctor. I suggest that you inform your physician as to exactly what type of exercise you're going to undertake, and that you not only have a physical but have him monitor you while you're undergoing this training. It's the procedure I followed, and I think anyone who does less is being foolhardy.

Other Successful Methods

If by chance your doctor forbids you to undertake stressful training, there are a great number of other ways that you can motivate yourself to be successful. The trick is to send yourself the right message. If you listen to the great motivators of the twentieth century—Zig Ziglar, Earl Nightingale, Dr. Norman Vincent Peale—they all send the same message: "You are what you think." You're a product of positive and negative conditioning. If you've been positively conditioned, you'll have a positive mental attitude and react positively to the world and succeed as a result. On the other hand, if as a result of your conditioning you have a negative mental attitude, you'll react negatively and you'll fail. Almost every successful person we interviewed agreed that a positive mental attitude was necessary for success. Our interviews with these successful people showed us that there is a whole variety of ways that you can develop a positive mental attitude. Brainwashing yourself may work for some but obviously won't work for everyone, and even if it works for you, there is no reason that you have to use one technique exclusively. In fact, most of the successful students we had combined several methods for the best results. The methods they used were wide and varied.

The best-known method, of course, is the motivational meeting at which you have a dynamic motivational speaker. Today the king of these motivational speakers is Zig Ziglar.

If you attend one of his presentations, there is very little chance that you will not want to get up and cheer, not if you surrender yourself to it and become involved in it. I've spoken on the stage with Mr. Ziglar on numerous occasions, and when I first did I was astounded at the response of the audience. In fact, the thing that really surprised me is that the same people come back time and again. Being a researcher, I started asking them why, and found that for many, Zig Ziglar is a motivational fix and keeps them going. He charges their psyches. A visit to Zig is like a visit to a resort. He restores people, he gets them ready to go out and give their all. As a result, attending his meetings has become necessary to his followers' success. If you've found your Zig Ziglar, I don't suggest you stop attending his meetings. What I do suggest is that you, in addition to attending his meetings, attempt other methods.

The second most popular motivational method used in America is the motivational tape. Men like Zig Ziglar, Norman Vincent Peale, and Dennis Waitley tape their messages, and sell these tapes to their followers. These people play the tapes on a regular basis as a source of inspiration, or they play them before important meetings, important sales calls, and important decisions. Our survey of people who use tapes tells us why they're so popular. For thousands and thousands, the tapes work beautifully. If they work for you, use them.

I could describe dozens of methods people have successfully used to motivate themselves, but knowing what works for others is not important. Apparently, any method that helps you absorb positive messages is good. Even if a method seems silly, if it works for you, use it. Subliminal-message devices are reported by many to work wonderfully. Some have suggested hypnosis. A number of people we interviewed said that posthypnotic suggestion was, for them, the key to top performance, and these people came from a variety of fields, from sales to engineering. And we all have heard of the rich and famous who depend on gurus for their motivation. I could never go that route, but if it works for them, I wouldn't tell them to look elsewhere.

There are even those who believe in a transfer of motivation, particularly from athletics. We spoke to numbers of marathon runners, swimmers, handball players who said that after a good game of tennis or a good run, or a good swim, or a terrific competitive experience, they were all charged up, ready to go back to the office and take on the world. Whether the physical experience simply relaxed them and let them recharge their mental batteries, or the sense of accomplishment related to physical activity acted as a source of motivation itself, I'm not sure. But I am sure that physical exercise works for many; if it works for you, use it.

Group Motivation

Obviously, if I weren't convinced that individuals could motivate themselves and change their lives as a result, I wouldn't have written this chapter. But I'm equally convinced, after interviewing several thousand people about how they got themselves started, that many are not capable of self-motivation, or find it extremely difficult. They are the social beings. They will die for their country, their company, the Marine Corps, or any one of hundreds of other groups. They are people who will work very productively because they believe it is their duty to be productive, and they believe this because they belong to a group that teaches that productivity is positive. They're good Christians, good Moslems, good Jews, and they usually find only group motivation compelling. Because there are millions of such people, it's absolutely critical, if America's going to compete successfully with the Japanese, that we adopt some of the Japanese methods, particularly the methods they use to indoctrinate and motivate their employees. Most Japanese employees start their days with light exercise, and heavy motivation. The companies either have songs, chants, or a list of company objectives that every employee is required to repeat every morning. It is this repetition of positive ideas that gives the Japanese worker an edge. Unless we motivate our workers in a similar way, there's no way they or we can compete.

CHAPTER THREE

Successful Workers

A Profile of Successful Workers

In 1976–77 while conducting research for an earlier book, *Live for Success*, my people questioned a thousand American executives and asked them if being a great worker would guarantee success. Nine hundred and twelve said it wouldn't, but it would make success possible since being a poor worker, in their opinion, guaranteed failure.

They also agreed that the one unifying thread that runs through the lives of most successful men and women is that they are good workers. A vast majority are also marathon workers. In fact, the overwhelming majority of successful men and women we interviewed attributed their success primarily to hard work. They told us they work long hours, and were dedicated too, and enjoyed their jobs.

However, there is a substantial percentage of very successful men and women who do not work very hard. In fact, there is even a percentage who do not believe in the work ethic. We ran across a surprisingly large number of men and women who work efficiently only for short periods of time, so that they can take vacations, spend time on their hobbies, or be with their families. A number of these successful people are professionals who run half a shop. There are attorneys who work only on cases that attract them, doctors who perform only operations that interest them, and men and women who run small private businesses on a part-time basis. Their present life-styles didn't come about as a result of a fortunate accident. Most of them at one time went to a great deal of trouble planning their businesses so that they could lie on the beach, play golf, race yachts, or follow their dreams. Although the image of the hard-working success-oriented driver is true in many cases, it's not true in all. The tie that binds both groups of successful people together is that when they work, they usually do more than their unsuccessful counterparts and invariably do it better.

Successful men and women start by approaching their jobs differently than do their less effective brothers and sisters. If you throw a job at them, they never dive right into it. First, they analyze. Whether they are in organizations or not, they're organization men and women. They're organized in everything they do. Once they get into a project, they throw themselves into it completely. They have enormous powers of concentration. If, in the middle of a job, they see they're going about it in the wrong way, they immediately call a halt and admit their mistake. They have self-confidence that allows them to look at themselves very critically.

If you speak to one of them for a few minutes, the first thing you will notice is that he or she exudes self-confidence. Eighty-three percent of those we questioned said that when they began in their field they could do almost any job as well as or better than people who'd been in the field for years, and that they have improved with time. They take great pride in this belief. Their motto, if they had one, would be the World War II motto "The difficult we do right away, the impossible takes a little longer"—and they would add that nothing seems impossible. No job is too big or too difficult. In fact, that's their secret. They enjoy challenges. Challenge excites them. The bigger the challenge, the greater the sense of excitement. While they want to conquer worlds, climb tall mountains, cure cancer, save great companies, or build them, they find no job too small, too menial, or too boring. Their excitement about their work doesn't come from the work, but from themselves. They're self-starters, and they generate their own sense of excitement by being totally committed to anything they undertake. Many of them are dedicated sports enthusiasts, and they put everything they have into that as well. They enjoy the company, friendship, and camaraderie of others who do the same, and despise people who put less than 100 percent effort into everything they do. It is this attitude that makes hard work so essential to success. You're not even going to get a chance to associate with the movers and shakers unless you're a worker, because they can't stand people who aren't.

A Comparison of Successful and Unsuccessful Workers

The greatest difference between those who work effectively and those who do not, unsurprisingly, is that those who work effectively enjoy it. If they're given a job or forced to do a job they find boring, dull, and tedious, they try to convince themselves it isn't; and if they can't convince themselves that the job they're working on is interesting, fun, and exciting, they make a contest out of it. If they had to push a peanut up a hill with their nose, they'd want to know the world's record for pushing a peanut up a hill. And even if they didn't have a chance of beating it, they'd like to know how close they could come. They live in a world that is full of challenges and contests, instead of obstacles and pitfalls. As a result, when they finish one job, they run looking for a new one, because each job is a challenge and a new game.

These successful people don't always succeed, but they never fail. If they lose today, it's only today's contest. There's always next year, next season, next week, next day, and the next five minutes. Since life is a series of challenges they expect to win, they can accept the occasional setback, but they never accept defeat, because they simply don't recognize it. Defeat for them is nothing more than a temporary setback, which they intend to correct.

Successful people especially stand out when you place them next to unsuccessful people, and that's exactly what we did. We surveyed 653 men and women who were identified by their superiors as very good workers, and 428 others working for the same companies, and many times in the same departments and the same jobs, who were identified as poor workers. The group was almost equally divided between men and women, and we interviewed some matched pairs: people in the same position, working at the same job, at the same level for about the same amount of time, one of whom was headed for bigger things, while the other was failing miserably. We also interviewed a number of top executives who were work superstars, to see how their comments related to those of good and poor workers. The most surprising fact that we uncovered is that good workers find going to work much easier. It takes much less effort for them to show up and do a great deal of first-rate work than it does in many cases for the poor workers to show up and do very little second-rate work. Good workers, as I mentioned before, are like great athletes: they complain about pain and effort; however, they take such pride in their accomplishments that pain and effort don't count. Their descriptions of how they feel when they finish an important job or find themselves at the top of the heap are very similar to the descriptions top athletes give of how they feel when they win a race or a game. With their attitudes, pain and suffering are turn-ons, not turn-offs. What they do is enjoyable because people who perform Herculean tasks, whether they're running marathons or completing great projects, have a sense of accomplishment, and their sense of accomplishment is enhanced by the fact that they suffered to reach their goals. Marathoners believe that if running a great marathon were easy, no one would want to do it. If you listen to great workers talk about work, they have the same belief about working: if it didn't take effort and skill, and if anyone could do it, they wouldn't be interested. They love working on the big case, or working to get the big promotion, or performing a very difficult operation, because, like great athletes, they believe that they are better people because they've accomplished something.

They also hold other beliefs that make it easier for them to work. We found that most successful people believe there is a direct correlation between how hard they work and their chance of being successful, while ineffective people generally believe that success is due to a variety of elements outside their control—luck, connections, etc. Therefore, they do not see the importance of working.

We also found there was a correlation between belief in the system and the ability to work for and succeed within the system. Those we interviewed who were effective, successful workers believed in free enterprise far more than the people who were not. They were not necessarily conservative politically, but they tended to lean in that direction. The conclusion I drew was not that belief in democracy and capitalism makes you more aggressive or more effective, but that it is easier to work for a system that you believe in than one you don't. It is my guess that the most effective workers in the Soviet Union are dedicated communists.

Not only were the good workers somewhat more enamored with the capitalistic system than were the general population, they were often head over heels in love with their own profession, and very loyal to it. We found more loyalty to their profession than to their company. Top engineers were proud of being engineers, and they usually had joined engineering societies. The same was true of top doctors, plumbers, lawyers, dentists, and every other group we questioned. In addition, they were more likely to socialize with people in their own fields, because they enjoyed the company of others who were engaged in their profession. And finally, they often encouraged their children to join their profession.

We went out of our way to interview successful men and women who said they wished they hadn't spent their lives in the field they were in or would like to go into something else. We expected their attitude to be as negative as those people who are nonproductive, but it wasn't. Most of them were simply bored with what they were doing after doing it for years. They often had climbed all the heights their field had to offer, and now they were looking for new horizons. They still talked with some excitement and passion about how they'd started. Most of them said there was a time when they were in love with their profession or job, and over 70 percent agreed that if you've never been in love with what you're doing, the chances are that you're not very good at it, and you're probably not going to succeed.

However, we did find people who didn't like what they were doing, and yet were very effective. They admitted they worked only for money. Their interest was in giving their families a good life-style, and for this they were willing to make the sacrifice of being effective in spite of hating their jobs. These people all said that they had been effective workers before they entered the field, and that they were effective in spite of it. It is my belief they would have been a lot more effective if they'd liked what they were doing. One of the main reasons I believe this is true is that these people were stingy with their time; most effective workers are not. They're not looking for shortcuts or an easy way out, and they are not particularly interested in going home at exactly five o'clock. They're willing to stay around until they think they've completed their job. In fact, one of the key differences between effective and ineffective workers is that they look at time differently. Ineffective workers wrote Parkinson's Law and they obey it. They let their job expand to fill the time given to do it, and conversely they will shove an hour-and-a-half job into a one-hour time segment if taking the time required to do it well interferes with anything they consider more important than work—and unfortunately they consider almost everything more important than work. Good workers, on the other hand, will do a job as quickly and as effectively as possible, and then they'll ask for something else. If there's nothing to do, they'll sit and read the paper. The one thing they hate to do, and many absolutely refuse to, is to pretend to work, which is what most poor workers do all the time. One of the saddest commentaries on American industry is that a substantial percentage of the people identified as effective workers told us they were fired or forced to leave jobs because they wouldn't fake working. Being effective got them into trouble.

Poor workers are not always slow workers. They speed up when it suits them, even though the quality of their work will suffer. They do enough to get by. If they plan it right, they do enough so that no one's going to fire them. They cut corners because cutting corners is a life-style with them. You might think that if they're given one hour's work and two hours to do it, the quality of the work would improve. It usually doesn't. They almost always do just enough to get by, or what they think will get them by, and never any more.

Some supervisors we spoke to identified the critical difference between good and poor workers in one phrase: *good enough*. They said good workers never use the phrase, and poor workers use it all the time. But whether poor workers use the phrase or not, it expresses their attitude toward work. Almost all agreed that good workers will perform at a high level if they're being observed. Good workers have tremendous pride, and if they think a third party is going to see their work, they will work very hard for the third party's approval. Good workers, we found in the opinion of most of the people around them, are far more social beings than poor workers. They may not seem to because they're not gabbing at the office all day, but they value the opinions of their co-workers. At the same time, most good workers will work even when they're not being observed, and when no one is going to see the work, because they have an internal guide that says only the best will do. And only the best will do because, as I pointed out earlier, every job is a contest and in every contest they must win.

Compete, Compete, Compete, Win, Win, Win

The word most often used by excellent workers to describe the job they did was *win*. They like being on a winning team, they like winning ways, they like a winning combination. They are winners, and they know they're winners, and they love other winners, and they despise losers. Good workers are competitors. They compete in everything they do. Competition is a way of life for them: they live, breathe, and dream competition. They can't stand to be number two; they want to be number one; there is nothing better than being number one. There's nothing that they like better than going head on with the best. They love to work for a small company that's about to take the number-one company apart. In fact, the only thing they enjoy more than being number one is beating number one. Their motto is *compete, compete, compete, compete, win, win, win, win.*

How They Use Daydreams

Even I didn't completely understand how essential competing and winning was to being an effective worker until I started asking about their daydreams. The reason the subject became part of my research is that many of the supervisors said that poor workers spend their lives daydreaming instead of working, and we set out to check the validity of this statement. We started asking good and poor workers about their daydreams. We found, unsurprisingly, that poor workers spend more time daydreaming than good workers. However, we discovered something very surprising: the nature of their daydreams is dramatically different.

Good workers use their daydreams as a form of planning. They often said they thought about projects that were in front of them. They play games with problems. Most of them believe, as I do, that if you become acquainted with a problem thirty days before you have to make a decision, even if you don't spend any time consciously working out your decision, you're far more able to deal with that problem because you've had it in your mind. We found that poor workers don't share this belief. They believe that the only time you work at a problem is when it's placed in front of you.

In addition to using their daydreams to solve problems, the good workers also fantasized. However, their fantasies often involved their work. They dreamed about getting a Pulitzer prize or a Nobel prize or making a break-through in their field. As a result, they not only derived a certain amount of enjoyment from daydreaming, but their daydreams acted as an added incentive for them to continue to work at whatever they were doing. In fact, two very successful scientists made almost identical statements; they said that their daydreams were "prerewards for work." One man said that when he finished a project, it was almost never as good as the daydream, and, since he'd already patted himself on the back and taken the reward, he felt obliged to go on and accomplish more.

Of course, unproductive workers daydream too. In fact, they daydream all the time, but the subjects of their daydreams differ dramatically from those of good workers' daydreams. Poor workers' dreams almost never involve work. They dream about vacations, sex, being heroic, and so on. Their daydreams distract them from work rather than involve them in it. The people who were very productive also daydreamed about sex and desert islands, but the work association often remained. I ran across two men, one a chemist and the other a physicist, both very effective and both very highly thought of in their fields, who described an almost identical recurrent daydream. In their shared daydream, each traveled to Stockholm to be awarded the Nobel prize. After receiving the prize, while still dressed in his tux and looking terrific, he was seduced by the most beautiful and glorious tall blonde that he'd ever seen. These men's daydreams were as sexy and as vivid as the daydreams of the unproductive, but in both cases their sexual fantasies were connected with their work, a characteristic that is common in productive people's daydreams.

We uncovered a very significant difference between good and poor workers when we asked them three questions: whether they wanted to improve, whether they thought they could improve, and how they would like to improve. Both groups wanted to improve. I think the poor workers gave more lip service to this than did the good workers, but I can't be sure. The most easily noticed difference was how they wanted to improve. The poor workers were mainly interested in improving the quantity of their work, while good workers were mainly interested in improving the quality. Poor workers wanted to finish fast so that they could go home. They showed a great interest in working a four-day week and a six-hour day. When we asked good and poor workers whether they thought productivity training could significantly increase their personal productivity, poor workers were generally unsure and negative, while good workers believed that productivity training not only could but would help them. While productivity training fascinated good workers, it obviously frightened poor ones.

There is one additional difference that I must mention. Good workers were usually happier, richer, and more successful than poor workers. If you want to join their ranks, read on.

CHAPTER FOUR

Helping Your Child Become a Super Worker

Productivity Is Important

I taught for eight years and during that time had at least fifty parents complain that I was too demanding a teacher. They did not think that their children should be required to spend several hours a night doing homework. They believed that childhood should be a carefree time, without work and without responsibility. Unfortunately, children raised without work and responsibility soon become adults who can't work and are irresponsible.

The first thing parents in this country must do is teach their children that productivity is important. I know we all give lip service to that ideal, but the fact is many of us do not live up to it. Productive children are the product of productive parents, or at least parents who teach the value of being productive in the home, who teach the value of hard work, and who equate hard work with success. Even if you don't believe that hard work is the key to success, teach this to your children, because our research shows that if your children don't believe that, they're less likely to succeed. We found that young people as well as older people who believe that hard work is necessary for success are more likely to be hard workers and to be successful than those who don't.

In our survey of high-school underachievers and over-achievers who had successful parents,* we found that when either parent praised the achievement, success, hard work, and dedication of the other parent, the children took this as a clue for forming their work habits. On the other hand, if either parent denigrated the achievement or hard work of the other parent, the children took that as their clue. Children generally perform those activities that produce pleasure. If parents ignore children, and tell the children that the reason they're ignoring them is they must work to succeed, those children won't work. Children who'd been treated this way told our researchers that they didn't wish to repeat the mistakes of their parents. If children see their parents' hard work as a source of pleasure, if Dad's or Mom's hard work is the thing that allows them to have a car, live in a better house, wear designer jeans, go to a better school, etc., then work is desirable and they will work.

They Will Do as You Do

As most parents know, children will not do as you say, they'll do as you do. Therefore, your children should see you working effectively. Since in most cases mothers dominate the raising of children, it is the mothers who are most often used as role models for work habits. Children use the father as a role model only when he works in their environment. We found when we interviewed children who are overachievers that the vast majority used their mothers

*Conducted during the 1981–82 school year.

as role models for their work habits. The only children who used their fathers were children who saw their fathers work. These were either fathers who took work home, or owned their own businesses. I believe this is one of the reasons that very successful fathers sometimes have children who are unsuccessful. If you're a successful male and your wife is not effective, and you want to help your children, take each child to work at least half a dozen times. Let them see you being very effective before they reach age twelve, because we found that in most cases by age twelve work habits and attitudes are firmly established.

While overachieving young people describe their mothers as being effective and efficient, underachievers describe the harried housewife. If any woman reading this book is constantly overwhelmed by her world, if she's constantly running as if she doesn't know where she's going, she's teaching her children the primary habit of failure. Children reason that if the world overwhelms Mother, there's no reason it shouldn't overwhelm them.*

You Can Do Anything

Another message that parents of overachievers send is "You can do anything." They send the message not only by telling their children that the only limits they have are those that are self-imposed, and that they expect them to do

---

*Before undertaking this research, we tested many interview methods on students and decided that peer interviews worked best, since students were very candid when they were talking to peers. Therefore, we hired high-school students to interview high-school students and junior-high-school students to interview junior-high-school students. I mention this here because much of the research done on young people, in my opinion, is totally invalid, since the interviews are conducted by adults, and, whether we adults would like to admit it or not, most young people look upon us as the enemy, and you don't tell the enemy the truth.

great things, but by acting as if they trusted them to do great things. Parents who allow their children to experiment, to take chances, to be responsible for their own actions, are really the only ones telling children they can do anything. Parents of successful children tell them over and over, "I trust you to be able to handle yourself." This allows children to develop into effective, efficient people. Overprotective parents produce inefficient underachievers, and underprotective parents produce inefficient children as well. Children whose parents don't set limits are convinced that their parents don't care, and this has a damaging effect upon their egos. Instead of believing they can do everything, they believe they can do nothing.

Rewards

Children react best when they're faced with specific rewards and punishments. Children who were identified as overachievers were invariably rewarded at home for achieving. Although the rewards took many forms, in reality there was only one reward—parental approval. Some parents gave children ten dollars for every A on their report card; others simply congratulated them and patted them on the back. We found that children check on parental approval by seeing if their parents really disapprove when they fall short. Every one of the overachievers we interviewed said that at one time they brought home a bad report card. After speaking to a dozen personally, I believe they brought home at least one poor report card just to see what would happen. Since in most cases the parents were enraged, annoyed, or disappointed, and showed their rage, annoyance, or disappointment, it was the last poor report card the child brought home. I believe if those parents in any way had accepted underachieving, that's what they would have gotten from that point on, because our interviews with underachievers indicated that their parents did accept failure. Being a too understanding parent is terribly destructive to a child's potential.

The other thing that can destroy children as workers is expecting too much. When the youngsters were interviewing other youngsters, they ran across numbers of students who said, "What's the point? I can't get an A. I'm not bright enough to get an A. I know that at best I'm a C student, but I get F's because C and F are the same to my parents. There's no point in my working because there's no way I can gain my parents' approval." In order to push your children you have to realistically understand what they're capable of doing. If you push them past the point where they're capable of performing, they'll stop performing completely, because if there's no difference in your mind between C and F, there will be no difference in theirs. If they can't possibly reach the goals you set for them, they will quit trying.

The Money Message

You have to be very careful about the messages you send to children because they take things quite literally, and as a result, many well-meaning parents send children exactly the opposite message they wish to. The most counterproductive message we ran across is the money message. Parents who in conversations equate only money with success and say that the only real reward in this world is money ironically often raise children who will never make much money. Children who believe the money message take part-time jobs after school, often with their parents' encouragement. They fill all the fast-food places in America, work in shoe stores, and do everything in their power to gain their parents' approval. They make money. The problem is, unless the money is needed to support the family, it's probably counterproductive money. When we interviewed high-school students, we found that most of those who had part-time jobs after school performed poorly in school. The reason is they understood their parents' message to be that earning money is more important then getting good grades. Their parents would tell them this is not true when they brought home their report card, but the message, as they read it, is that it is more important to earn a minimum wage than to get an A in algebra. As a result, they set out to do exactly what they think their parents want, usually to the dismay of their parents. One of the great myths in this society is that putting a child in a real job that pays real money will lead to success. We found this is not true. We found that children do not learn to work effectively in minimum-paying jobs. What they learn in most cases is to do as little work as possible, or to do enough to get by. Minimum-paying jobs exist mostly in the world of least-common-denominator productivity. It's work when the boss is watching, and goof off when he isn't. Unfortunately, our interviews indicated that young people often carry this information back to their academic life. If your child's first real work experience is a minimum-paying job, he's probably getting antiproductivity training. I even question the value of students having summer jobs, although there doesn't seem to be a correlation between students holding summer jobs and their ability to perform as workers or as students.

The reason I put such emphasis on young people's ability to work in school is that there's a very high correlation between good students and top workers. Our interviews with top workers indicated that they were almost always good students. By good students, I do not mean straight-A students, and by poor students I don't mean F students, although they may have gotten those marks. By good students, I mean those who did their homework, had it in on time, were responsible in the classroom, and didn't cause any trouble; and by poor students, I mean youngsters who didn't do their homework, didn't hand in their assignments on time, and were always in trouble. There are exceptions to the rule, but they're not many. We found that people who worked very hard in school worked very hard at work, and people who didn't work in school don't work in business. In addition, we found that parents who sent the message through their daily activities and conversations that education was critical, and that they valued it above social and sports success, had children who were hard-working, effective, and productive. The message must be given in the first three to four grades of school, and it's very important to send a clear message.

A Productive Homework System

Our interviews with effective and ineffective workers and with students who were identified as overachievers and underachievers led us to one inescapable conclusion. Parents' attitudes toward homework was the critical factor in the academic success of their children. Parents who checked on and worked with their children at home were much more likely to have effective, efficient, productive students who would become effective, efficient, and productive adults. Again, it wasn't simply giving lip service to homework; it was active participation in the homework by parents that turned out effective students. The most effective students were generally those whose parents asked them what homework they had, checked on their homework, and, if they were able, sat down and helped them with it. They were not parents who sat down and did the homework for their children.

One of the most interesting facts is that effective students who became effective workers almost always did their homework in the center of the family unit. The favorite place for effective students to do homework, particularly in their younger years, was at the kitchen table. When it was cleaned off after supper, it became the homework place. The parents helped, watched, oversaw, and showed an interest in the homework. Very seldom were over-achievers sent to their room to do their homework. Students in grades one through eight who worked in their rooms were generally ineffective students who would later in life become ineffective workers. Apparently, young people learn to work by working under supervision. The better the supervision in early years, the more effectively they worked then and would in adult life.

We found when we questioned effective workers who came from nonacademic backgrounds that they worked at home as well; they had chores. These workers were su-pervised as young people, and nothing but perfection or close to perfection was accepted. They were allowed to do nothing less than their best. The reason they did their best is that they were not sent off to do something on their own. Their parents checked on them, whether they were sent to clean their rooms or do another chore. The parents demanded at least to see the end product, and often they were involved in the process. They would yell at a young-ster for not cleaning the room properly as the youngster was doing it, and if he did not know how to clean a room, they'd show him how. They would make the youngster go back and improve his or her work, often while they watched. Ineffective workers said that as young people they were sent off to do their chores and never checked on, which means that if you want your child to be a good worker, you must teach him how to work.

CHAPTER FIVE

Measuring Your Work

Your Personal Productivity Chart

The first question that most people I meet at cocktail parties ask me is how long it takes me to write a book. My answer is always the same. My books take several years to research and several months to put into readable form. I'm not William Shakespeare; I'm a professional pop-science writer, and I can take research material and put it into a digestible form in a relatively short period of time. Therefore, it is ironic that this book, which deals with productivity, has been years in preparation, and that I've been working on this chapter for more than ten months.

The reason that this chapter took so long is that the earlier versions didn't work. I finished the first draft in lightning speed—it took me less than two days. As I always do with new work, I gave it to my friends and asked for their opinions. They unanimously agreed it was terrific, and said they enjoyed reading it. In fact, two were so enthusiastic that they decided to act on its advice right away. They set out to create their own personal productivity charts and to improve their productivity immediately, without waiting for the remainder of the book. The problem was that each of them believed his job was so unique that the chapter as it stood wouldn't work for him. Each asked me to personalize the chapter so that he could use it. The minute they made the request, a horrible thought struck me. If these two very intelligent men working in middle-American industry in quite ordinary jobs found it impossible to follow the instructions in the chapter, how many others would have the same difficulty?

Being a researcher, I ran a little test. I arranged to have the chapter read by twenty-eight men and fourteen women selected randomly in the Wall Street area. To my consternation, 33 percent of them found it difficult, if not impossible, to follow the instructions in the chapter, which meant that the chapter, as it stood, did not work. A self-help book that raises more questions than it answers isn't worth the paper it's written on, so I edited and rewrote.

Unfortunately, after half a dozen edits and rewrites, I still had a chapter that didn't work. Although each subsequent version tried to answer the questions raised by the earlier one, the number of questions continued to grow, and the chapter only became longer, not better.

I had just about given up on finding a satisfactory format, which meant, since this was a critical chapter, that this book would never be completed, when my three-and-a-half-year-old son solved the problem for me. He threw his ball over a chain-link fence, very lazily walked up to the gate, put his little feet into the holes, climbed to the top, and, while holding on with one hand, leaned over and unlocked the very tricky gate mechanism. He then climbed down, opened the gate, and walked through. My first reaction was not, "Eureka, I've got the solution to my problem," but, "Oh, no, he can open the gate to the swimming pool." My wife and I never thought that he'd be able to climb to the top of the fence and unlock that very tricky latch. I called him over and asked him how he learned to open the gate, and he said, in an annoyed, matter-of-fact tone, that the lock on the fence was the same as the lock on his toy box, and since he could open his toy box, he could open the fence. He realized, if I didn't, that if you solve a problem in one environment the solution is likely to work in another. I would have missed the solution even then, except that, when it dawned on him that I was amazed by his feat, he immediately became very proud of it and told everyone. After about the sixth telling, I realized that he had solved my problem. All I had to do was to move a solution from one environment to another.

I had been giving courses on productivity to small groups of employees for some time. With the first group, after I spent an hour explaining how to fill out a personal productivity chart, I had to spend two additional hours explaining what I really meant. Although I had the same problem with the second group, by the time I ran the third group I had solved it. When people asked the same questions, I pulled out the forms filled out by the first two groups, and used them to answer the questions. In a few minutes the old charts seemed to answer all the questions. That is why at the end of this chapter you will find several completed personal productivity charts. After you've read them and the supporting material, you should have no problem filling out your own.

Before looking at a completed personal productivity chart, it is necessary to understand its different elements. The present personal productivity chart is really a combination document. Originally, I had my students fill out three separate charts: a simple flow chart to let them know how they spend their time, an interruption chart on which they recorded when and by whom or what they were interrupted, and, finally, a performance chart on which they graded the quality and quantity of their work, and made comments about how they might improve.

The reason I combined the three charts is that I found

there were correlations among the type of work assigned, the number of times people allowed themselves to be interrupted, and, of course, the quantity and quality of work produced. Since these relationships exist, it is more useful to have all the information compiled at one time, and it is even helpful to have it all on one sheet of paper. In addition, keeping one chart speeded up the training. While originally my employees spent up to ninety days keeping records before attempting improvement, I found that with the combined chart they could start improving their performance after twenty to twenty-five days of measurement.

Ideally, you should keep personal productivity charts for six weeks; but if you find yourself pushed for time, you can start your improvement training after four weeks.

The headings on the personal productivity chart look self-explanatory. But they're not, because this chart is really several charts combined, and, if it is to be useful, you're going to have to record several types of information in each column.

Recording Your Jobs

For example, although the heading of the first column is Jobs, we want you to record not only what you're doing, but where you're doing it. We found that where people work often has a profound effect on how well they work. In fact, in some cases it proved to be the critical factor— that is certainly true of college students. Many of the young people who work for me as researchers are full-time students. After I trained a number of them to perform more effectively as researchers, several asked me if I would help them apply my productivity techniques to their schoolwork. After being badgered for several months, I finally

JOHN T. MOLLOY'S
PERSONAL PRODUCTIVITY
CHART

Job	Time	Source of Interruption	Time Wasted	% My Fault	Additional Time Wasted	Comments, Quality & Quantity Score

undertook a study on how to improve the productivity of my employees as students. I discovered that many of the students who worked for me were most productive when they worked in the school libraries, and least productive when they worked in the dormitories. But a general rule based on that discovery would have been counterproductive, because I also discovered that for about 22 percent of the students the reverse was true: they were very productive when they worked in dormitories, and very unproductive when they worked in the library. When we questioned both groups, we saw why. The two groups had different study techniques. The students who memorized by repeating aloud naturally worked better in the dormitory since they couldn't talk aloud in the library, and without this ability, they were lost.

I found similar results when I worked with half a dozen contractors. While four of the six were far more effective at estimating bids in the home office, because there they had their supplies, information, telephone, and a quiet environment in which to think and figure, one of the six was only effective when he worked in the field. He was a person whose work style let him function best under pressure. We found that when he ran to a job, looked it over quickly, and did an on-the-spot estimate, he was far more accurate and his jobs were far more profitable than when he sat down and worked at bidding for hours. We also found that for one of the six it didn't make any measurable difference where he worked; he did as well in either environment.

I know the majority of people reading this book believe that where they work isn't an important factor, because they think that they have no choice about where they work. The fact is that almost everyone has a choice. The first and most obvious choice is which type of work you take home. Since almost everyone is obliged to take work home at different times, which work you select to do at home can be critical. Twelve percent of the people who finished work-flow charts decided that they were not taking the right work home. In addition, in most office settings there are several environments. We spoke to several attorneys who said that when they wanted to get something done, they went into the library. A number of top executives said they had similar hideouts or escapes, and for about 70 percent of them, using these hideouts was productive. But, surprisingly, for about 20 percent of them it was counterproductive—which means that almost 20 percent of them were putting efforts into being more productive and actually defeating their purpose.

Very subtle differences in your environment can have a major impact on it. If you can have your telephone calls held and insist that you not be interrupted, it dramatically changes your work environment. Therefore, when you're recording the place you work, we'd like you to indicate as much as you can about the place, and particularly whether you're likely to be interrupted or not when working there.

When recording place, it isn't necessary to write *home, office, field;* it's better to put the first letter of each location. I suggest you abbreviate not only here but throughout your chart. Otherwise keeping the chart could become so ponderous that it interferes with your work. In addition, abbreviation will keep your chart private. This is particularly important when filling out the Source of Interruption column. When you record interruption, be sure not to write people's real names or their initials. If George or Mary notice that their names or their initials are in your Interruption column, in all probability this will affect the number of times they interrupt you, and as a result can invalidate the entire process, or may create hard feelings and make it difficult for you to work with them in the future. Therefore you should abbreviate, or, even better, develop a simple code to identify sources of interruption; but be sure the code is very simple and self-evident, or that you keep a written record of it. We've had a number of people who went back after six months and couldn't identify the source of interruption, because they couldn't remember their code.

The second type of information you must record in the Job column is the name of the project. This will vary from individual to individual, and from job to job. For example, most attorneys list their jobs with the names of their cases: Jones vs. Jones, Smith vs. Smith. Contractors list their jobs by who paid them: Jones, Smith, General Motors, IBM, and so on. I find myself listing my jobs in two categories—who's paying for the job (corporation X, corporation Y) and the nature of the job (researching corporate image, researching uniforms, lecturing, and so on). There is only one rule on how to list your jobs: list them in a way that makes sense to you. The only person who has to read or understand this chart is you, and the only reason you're describing your job is so that you'll know how you're spending your time.

The third and final type of information you will need to record in this column is the type of activity in which you're involved. For example, most attorneys spend a significant amount of time in each of the following areas: clerical work, working with computers, negotiating and writing contracts. If you're an attorney, you must list each one of these separately. If you're a school teacher, you probably spend time preparing your classes, teaching, and correcting papers. Again, each function should be listed separately. Obviously, there are too many jobs and too many functions for me to even attempt to list them all. You have to make the decision as to how to divide your work. The only thing that's necessary for you to know is that the more detailed your division and the more information recorded, the more useful the chart. There is only one way to answer the question as to how much information should be recorded, and that is for you to apply the rule of common sense.

You'll use the second column to keep Time. Before you start recording Time, you have to understand how it affects the items in the first column. If you're an office worker, and as part of your job you go to the files, take out a file, read it for three minutes, go to the computer for two minutes, make one telephone call, and then make a decision, you'd go absolutely crazy if you tried to record when you started and finished each of those activities. It would be meaningless to have eight hundred little notations for each day's work. I recommend that you list only meaningful and measurable segments of time—those activities that take long enough so that you can give yourself a meaningful quality grade. Again, common sense is the rule. It's obvious that there is no way you can give yourself a meaningful grade if you walk over to a computer, hit a few buttons, and take information from it. If you go to that computer fifty times a day, you should note the number of visits and ask yourself at the end of the day whether you know enough about the operation and working of that computer, but don't list each visit.

If you're still confused as to which element you should list, I suggest that you start by listing them all, but only keep a permanent record of those segments of work that take at least five minutes, and to which you can give quality and quantity scores. I suggest that you list separately any segment that takes fifteen minutes, whether you can score it or not, and that you make it a point of listing any segment of work that has a critical effect on your ability to perform an essential function. For example, even though a stockbroker spends only a few minutes making decisions on how to invest during a week when something dramatic happens in the market, it certainly would be worthwhile for him to spend a great deal of time analyzing how well he performs that critical function, and how he might perform it more effectively. If, however, he spends a few minutes every week going to the files, he'd be wasting his time to even consider how he could do that more effectively. Becoming 50 percent more effective at that really wouldn't have any major effect on his productivity or his ability to perform his job.

As you may have guessed by now, the reason I call this a personal productivity chart is that the decisions about what to measure are personal, which means you must make decisions and judgments about your work, even though the decisions are often difficult and the judgments subjective. It is important that you make them. We found that the greatest improvement took place when individuals were forced to judge themselves. Supervisors, even the best of them who know exactly what is involved in your job, in most cases can only measure the appearance of productivity. The most sophisticated manager can only see the end product, and cannot see the internal mechanisms that go into its production. We questioned many employees who were described by their bosses as being very effective, who privately admitted that they spent most of their time goofing off. Your boss cannot look into your mind and explore your innermost thoughts, and that is what is necessary if you are going to have meaningful improvement, and that is exactly the object of a personal productivity chart.

As a result, it will be much more accurate than the productivity charts made by third parties, because it lays bare your soul, and for that reason it's absolutely critical that your chart be kept private. Only under such conditions will most people honestly record how much effort they put into a job, and how well they really did. Even so, filling out this chart accurately, even when you're the only one who's going to read it, will require courage.

Naturally, individual differences will and should affect how a person fills out the chart. I worked with two attorneys in the same office who, as far as I could see, were doing the same job. The first attorney divided preparation time into interviewing and preparation. The second attorney divided preparation time into interviewing, taking notes, library work (in which he included any work where he used reference books), time spent on the computer, taking depositions, and rewriting. At the end of three months both they and their superiors agreed that they had dramatically increased their effectiveness. Since I had both men in the same room at the same time, I asked them if they would mind comparing charts. I wanted to know why they were so dramatically different. After each looked at the other's chart, both immediately came to the same conclusion—that each person's own chart was probably right for himself. The first attorney said that if he had tried to divide his work into those small segments, it would have interfered with his getting his work done. The second insisted that dividing the chart as the first attorney did would be meaningless for him. Although both were correct, the man who divided the information into smaller segments learned more from the chart and had a greater increase in productivity. Since this is true in most cases, we suggest that you keep as detailed a personal productivity chart as you can, at least for the first two or three weeks.

Recording Time

The second column of the personal productivity chart is headed Time. Note the time whenever something meaningful happens—when you start a job, when you finish it, when you lay it down for a few minutes, or when you're interrupted. The first time we want you to record is not when you start working, but when you begin your day. I suggest that you start your personal productivity chart when you get up in the morning and end it when you go to bed at night. You should record every waking minute for at least the first three to four weeks. The reason I insist that you measure a full day and not just your working day is that you may decide that you're working at the wrong time, or at least doing the wrong type of work at the wrong time. Eighty percent of those who fill in this chart come to one conclusion or the other. I have an architect friend who acted as a guinea pig and helped me develop this chart. After filling it out for three weeks, he decided he did most of his creative thinking early in the morning before he arrived at the office with all its distractions. His work-flow chart showed him that he read *The New York Times* for about half an hour every morning on his way in on the train from Long Island, and that he usually worked on his way home at night. He decided to reverse this procedure. He started working in the morning and reading the *Times* in the evening. After two months he reported that he was far more productive than he had been before without adding one minute to his day. After a year he decided this was the most important decision he had made in the last five years.

I made a similar discovery when I analyzed my own chart. It had been my habit when writing a chapter for a book, or a column, or a report for a corporation to attempt to complete the assignment in one day, if that were at all possible. I believed that if I worked with information without walking away from it, I had a greater grasp and a better overview of the problem. After looking at my work-flow chart, I changed my mind. I saw that I did my best planning and was most creative at the end of the day. I also noticed that I was able to write most effectively and had fewer problems with rewrites when I produced my original copy in the morning. I changed my procedures as a result of these observations. Now I try to do my thinking and planning late in the evening and start writing as soon as I get up. This change alone has made me much more productive.

Obviously, if you're going to be keeping a log of everything you do during the day, it makes it much easier to have a clock or watch on your desk. If you don't have one, get one. Once you do you'll have no problem recording the jobs that go well. However, you will face a problem when you start a job at 9:02 that should take no more than thirty minutes, and look up again and find that it's 10:14 and you haven't finished. You'll be forced to ask yourself some very difficult and sometimes embarrassing questions—like what happened to the other forty-two minutes. If you leave that off, your chart falls apart. You must guess at how much time was wasted. All our subjects agreed that the best estimates are those made as soon as a job is finished. Let us assume that you started a job at 9:00, and all of a sudden you look up and it's 10:00, and you don't know where most of the time went. You should attempt to reconstruct what you've done. Let us assume that you thought you started working at 9:00 and you worked until 9:15 or so before you were interrupted, and then you had a series of small interruptions, and rather a substantial one between 9:30 and 9:45. If this is the best guess at how you spent your time, record it and put the letter E next to it. This will let you know, when you're reviewing your chart a month or a year later, that those times and reasons are estimates.

It is as important to record estimated times and reasons for work as it is to record actual times and reasons, because one of the easiest ways to increase your productivity is to eliminate nonproductivity lapse times. Lapse time is a hiatus in production that usually takes place at the same place and the same time every day. Another reason that recording estimated times is so important is that it's during these repeated productivity lapses that you're most likely to forget how much time you lost and what you were doing. Once you have recorded when and where productivity lapses have taken place, you can set up a program of eliminating the conditions that produce the lapses.

You will in most cases find it simple to eliminate most of them.

Recording the Sources of Interruption

In the third column I want you to record all sources of interruption. You need to know who or what interrupts you and when. There are several sources of interruption of course—people, things, procedures, and self. When you first start filling in your chart, pay very careful attention to the things that interrupt you: loud noises at the next desk, telephones ringing, explosions outside, elevators stopping by your floor, etc. The reason you want to be so careful to list things first is that they're the simplest items to eliminate.

Second, list procedures, things that happen in your office with a certain amount of regularity: the coffee machine coming by, people walking through the office, lights blinking on and off at night, the hum of the computer, talking to your fellow office employees, and so on. In this procedures category we would like you to list any source of *continual* interruption. For example, if they're constructing an office building next to you and they set off explosions every few minutes, it would be silly to record every time you heard an explosion. What you should do is write on the side of the column "From 8:00 in the morning to 5:00 at night, explosions." Follow the same procedure if two hours every morning there's a conference held in the next office and the people's voices distract you. Note that on your personal productivity chart. Although there's probably nothing you can do about the construction, maybe there's something you can do about the conference. You could, for example, arrange to be elsewhere when the conference is going on, or arrange to do your calling at that time so that your ear against the telephone blocks out the noise.

Third, make sure you list all the people who interrupt you. List everyone, whether it's their fault or yours. You must record whether the person interrupts you personally or in other ways. You should record every time someone calls you, and you must differentiate between someone calling you and you calling them. The simplest way to do it is to put a T in front of the name of the person if you call them, and a T after the name if they call you. Make sure you record who called: there's a major difference between calling a business associate and calling your bookie. You should also list the type of calls you accept, and when. If someone is supposed to be screening your calls and is still putting them through, it's a very simple thing to correct.

And, finally, you must of course record every time you interrupt yourself, when your mind drifts out the window and your concentration is broken, when you no longer can hold an idea or when you want to get up and go to the lavatory, wash your hands, stretch, look around. It doesn't make any difference what the reason—record it. Most of you are going to find that this is the area in which you record the most interruptions and where the interruptions are most deadly, and it is this area that will take the most work. Therefore, you must very carefully record all interruptions.

Time Wasted

The next three columns must be discussed together because they really deal with the same subject. The heading for the first is Time Wasted, the heading for the second is Percentage My Fault, and the heading for the third is

Additional Time Wasted. In the Time Wasted column record when someone comes over to your desk, even when he spends only a minute or two, no matter what the reason; record the person's name, when he came, the amount of time he spent.

Before you record in the next column, you must make a judgment. You must decide what percentage of the wasted time you're responsible for. If your boss calls you into his office and you spend a half hour without getting anything done, record that, indicating in the next column that you had no responsibility for that loss of time. There is no realistic way you can tell your boss you don't want to go into his office, even if you know it will be a waste of time. However, if your secretary comes to your desk and spends a half hour when five minutes would be adequate, you are 100 percent responsible for that twenty-five-minute loss in productivity, because you should be in control. There are times when both parties are totally responsible for time wasted. If you meet your friend at the water fountain and you stand there and talk for ten minutes, both of you know exactly what you're doing and you're both 100 percent responsible, because either of you can cut off the conversation. However, if you meet your boss at the water fountain and he starts talking about the football game last night, it's a bit more difficult to walk away from him than it is from one of your co-workers, and you're less responsible for that loss of time, even though you enjoy the conversation and partake in it just as enthusiastically. You have to be honest when estimating your percentage of fault, or the chart won't work.

The last of the three time columns is headed Additional Time Wasted. Although on some of the sample charts you will see at the end of the chapter this column is not filled out properly, it should be. It is often the most important column in the chart, because it can show you which interruptions are most deadly, and at which times interruptions are most deadly. For example, if your secretary comes over to your desk and spends five minutes she shouldn't and it takes you another five minutes to get back to work, she's wasted ten minutes of your time. The second five minutes should be reported in this column. There are times during your workday when a thirty-second interruption can cost you several hours of work. If you're attempting to solve a very complicated problem one afternoon and someone breaks your train of thought, it can be more destructive than going to the beach on another afternoon. There are interruptions that are so critical, the amount of time lost is almost incalculable. Nevertheless, you must guess. I remember working on a research design problem for weeks and finally coming up with the solution when the phone rang and broke my train of thought. I've never been able to recall that solution. To this day I can't remember it, and it irks me. This column will help you identify which type of activities are most affected by interruptions, and at which stages in particular projects you should cut off the phone and shut the door.

Comments, Quality and Quantity Score

The last column has a double heading, Comments, Quality and Quantity Score. At the end of each section of meaningful work, you must try to give yourself two grades: one for quality and the other for quantity. On occasions, both quality and quantity grades will be impossible. If you file one hundred sheets of paper in the filing cabinets and all you have to know is the alphabet to put them away, it's very difficult to give yourself a quality grade. We have to assume that you're going to put everything in the right place. It is equally difficult to give yourself a quantity grade on a critical decision. The only important thing is the quality. How much time you spend preparing to make a decision is not something you wish to measure; it's the quality of the decision you wish to measure. Therefore, there are times when you will only give yourself one grade, and there may be times when no grade will be possible. Again, this is a personal decision. Another problem my trainees told me they had was that it was always difficult for them to grade themselves. As a result, I came up with a system that makes it easy. Over a period of years I found that if I asked my trainees to think of the toughest and best teachers they ever had and to assume those teachers were giving them marks, they were able to come up with a consistent set of marks. Since the entire point of grades is to have a starting point at which you can realistically measure your improvements, consistency is the key. It's easiest if the teacher you use as a model is one who trained you in the field in which you are presently working: if you're an accountant, your most demanding accounting professor; if you're an attorney, your toughest, most demanding law professor; and so on. There are people for whom this will not work. If you're a salesperson or bricklayer or anyone working in a field for which there is no academic training, you will not be able to do this. What I suggest is that you think of your toughest and most demanding boss, and assume that he's going to grade you in the way your toughest high-school or college teacher did, and use that grade instead.

Use numerical grades, and be consistent. Give yourself 65 for passing work, 75 for average work, 85 for good work, 90 for very good work, 95 for exceptional work, and anything over that only for extraordinary work. At the end of each assignment, assume that that tough teacher or boss is standing over you and has been watching you work, with the ability to look into your mind and know everything about how you've completed your assignment, including how much effort you put into it. Then have the person give you one of those tough grades.

The comments that we ask you to record in the last column are two types, Immediate and Reflective. Immediate Comment is the comment you make when you finish a job. If you see something you could have improved, if you think the job was meaningless or stupid, write it down then and there. The reason we want you to make immediate comments is that a month later you won't remember what you thought when you finished the job.

The Reflective Comment, which can be very useful, is a later evaluation. Let us assume you complete a job after three weeks. It would be helpful if you went back through your personal productivity chart, looked at every aspect of the job, and made additional comments. Now that you know what the finished product is like, you'll be able to comment much more intelligently on how effectively you handled each part of the job. For example, you might go back to the day when you gave yourself a 90 because you thought you did a wonderful job, and realize that what you did that day didn't work. You might also look at Monday's work, which you thought deserved a grade of only 80, and decide that you really did your best work, and it should be a 99. That type of reflective comment can help you perform better in the future, particularly if you run across the same type of job. Everyone should be a Monday-morning quarterback if they have to play the same game again.

Sample Charts

As I stated in the beginning of this chapter, we're going to look at half a dozen personal productivity charts with the hopes that they will answer your questions before they crop up. In addition to showing you copies of the charts, I'm going to attempt to run through an explanation of each one, because we found this cleared up most questions. Please keep in mind these are not ideal charts. Ideal charts are filled out accurately and completely. The purpose of these charts is to show you how much they can vary and still be effective.

The first chart (see page 73) is that of a very effective attorney, and his first notation is "Smith vs. Jones, Review file." He indicates he started work at 8:51; at 9:03 his secretary brought coffee. He wasted only a minute. I think the 9:03 should be down another line, because if he were reading this chart a month later, he might think he started reviewing the file at 9:03 and the secretary was involved. Always drop the time to an empty space. At 9:10 we have a client interview. We don't know what he did for several minutes between 9:03 and 9:10; presumably he drank his coffee, or went back to reading the file. The more detail you put in your chart, particularly in the beginning, the better. At 9:20 the telephone rang—one minute lost. He doesn't indicate whether he made the call or if someone called him. Again, lack of information makes interpretation more difficult, and improvement more difficult. At 9:32, his secretary brought additional material, time wasted was three minutes. Walk a client to the door at 9:40, manners, time wasted was two minutes. Notation: "Necessary." He didn't give himself a score for that undertaking. At 9:43 he began reading a contract. Apparently the interview brought questions up in his mind, and he read the contract from 9:43 until 10:20, with one interruption at 9:50. Someone called him. He only spent a minute on the phone, but it wasted an additional ten minutes. Apparently it took him a while to get back to reading the contract, a very important piece of information; then he scored himself, 85 and 92. (I suggest that for the first two weeks you write "Quality" and "Quantity" next to each score just to make sure you get into the habit of doing them in the right order. We've had people who couldn't remember which score was which

Job	Time	Source of Interruption	Time Wasted	% My Fault	Additional Time Wasted	Comments, Quality & Quantity Score
Smith vs. Jones Review file	8:51 9:03	Secre-tary— Coffee	1 Min.	100%	0 min.	Necessary
Client interview	9:10 9:20 9:32	Telephone Secretary	1 3	0 0	0 0	Bring add. material
Bring client to door	9:40	Manners	2	0	0	Necessary
Read con-tract	9:43 9:50	Telephone	1	0	10	
Finished	10:20					Quality—85 Quantity—92
Called A.J.	10:22	Telephone	—	—	—	
Hang up	10:33					
Made notes	10:33 10:45	—	—	—	—	
Work— Brown	10:45 10:50 11:11 11:24 11:28 12:02	Telephone Telephone Telephone Telephone Mind drift	2 2 1 18 10	0 0 0 20 100	10 10 3 — 7	Had to take Had to take Had to take
	12:14 12:32 12:38 12:40 12:42 12:56	Files Lost letter Telephone I called	11 5 6 3	100 100 0 0	— 2 0 0	Should have asked sec. for files before she left for lunch. Organize desk.
Lunch	1:20					
Back	3:04					
Re-dictat-ing	3:18 3:31					Quality—90 Quantity—85
	4:26	Mind drift	4	100	0	
Hold calls	4:49	Sec.—let-ter	1	100	5	Don't interrupt Quality—82 Quantity—95

two months later.) At 10:22 he called A.J.; at 10:33 finished the call. He made notes from 10:33 to 10:45. He didn't give himself a score, but possibly didn't consider it important.

At 10:45, "Work—Brown." He said when I interviewed him about his chart that he would always know that that was work on the Brown case, that it was his form of shorthand. Although we recommend that you record as much detail as possible, if the Brown case is an essential part of your life, "Work on Brown" is adequate, since you'll know what it stands for two or three years later. However, don't write "Work—Jones" if you're only going to work on the Jones case for one hour, because you may forget who Jones was. You have to record more details about unimportant things than important ones. Notice that this subject worked on the Brown case from 10:45 until 1:20, when he went to lunch. During that time he took four telephone calls and two of them disturbed him quite a bit. In fact, he estimated that he lost ten extra minutes after both of these calls, but his comment was "Had to take," which meant he wasn't responsible for the wasted time. At 12:14 he noted files: time wasted was eleven minutes, and he was 100 percent responsible. "Should have asked sec. for the files before she left for lunch," was his comment. Obviously, he decided he had made a mistake in his procedure with his secretary. At 12:32 he lost a letter, had to organize desk; and at 12:42 he had another incoming telephone call for six minutes.

He telephoned out at 12:56, and up to this point his chart, with a few minor flaws, was very effective. But between 1:20 and 3:04 he went to lunch. When we questioned him about this chart thirty-two days after he drafted it, he couldn't remember what he did at lunch. He should have noted it. At 3:04 he came back and redictated something on the Brown case from 3:18 to 3:31. He gave himself grades of 90 and 85. At 4:49 he told his secretary he didn't wish to be interrupted. When we asked him why, he said it was because the interruptions in the morning were so damaging. This is a major flaw in this chart. You should wait at least two or three weeks before making any changes in your work procedure. I suggest you make no substantive changes until you finish your chart. This person made changes based on one morning's work. This is the main problem we see with people who start doing work-flow charts. They think they see their flaws right away, when in fact it takes two to three weeks before the severity of faults become evident. Look before you leap.

The second chart starts, "Smith vs. Smith." (See page 76.) This is an afternoon session with the same attorney on a different day. He has "Smith vs. Smith, 3:06 to 3:10, William asked for advice." Apparently William is another attorney. He considered all the time wasted and went back to his work at 3:26. "Tell H.": he couldn't remember several weeks later who H. was. At 3:43 he went to the library, and at 3:47 he began researching. Apparently it took a few minutes to walk there. At 4:01 his mind drifted and he indicated he wasted a few minutes. He went to the computer at 4:07 and apparently returned at 4:16; he doesn't say why, but he does indicate in his comment "Become better user." Re-record, 4:16 and 4:22. First draft, 4:23 to 4:52. Rewrite, 4:52 to 5:37. Rewrite again, 5:38 to 6:18, and then he has "Take it home." He gave himself scores in each of these letters, and I don't really think the scores are appropriate. I think you should score yourself only on a final product. If you rewrite a document several times, you may give yourself a very low score on quantity because you spent too much time on it, but a high score on quality. It is not necessary to keep several scores.

The third chart belongs to a manager of an engineering firm (see page 77). His first notation is that he arrived at 8:43, and his second is that he read a report at 8:50. He went on to his mail at 9:01; at 9:02 he has "Tell

Job	Time	Source of Interruption	Time Wasted	% My Fault	Additional Time Wasted	Comments, Quality & Quantity Score
Smith vs. Smith	3:06					
Read contracts	3:10	William asked for advice	17	0	3	
	3:26	Tell H.	4	0	5	
Library Start research	3:43					
research	3:47					
	4:01	Daydreaming	3	100	2	
Computer	4:07					
	4:16					Become better user
Re-record	4:16					
	4:22					
Write first draft of letter	4:23					
	4:52					40, 60
Rewrite	4:52					
	5:37					50, 70
Rewrite	5:38					
	6:18					50, 50
Take it home						

W." He knew who W. was a month later. It's probably easier for someone who works in an office with the same people every day to use little abbreviations to describe who he's dealing with. It's even possible for you to use initials that have nothing to do with the names if you want to disguise information on your work chart, but if you're dealing with different people every day, it's probably best to use the real name and write it out. From 9:08 until 9:16 he dictated two letters, and he gave himself two scores, 80 on quality and 90 on quantity. From 9:16 until 9:24 he got papers for a meeting. At 9:30 the meeting started; it went until 11:52. He gave himself 70 for quality, but doesn't give

Job	Time	Source of Interruption	Time Wasted	% My Fault	Additional Time Wasted	Comments, Quality & Quantity Score
Arrive	8:43					
Read report	8:50					
Mail	9:01					
	9:02	Tell W.	1	100	—	
Dictates 2 letters	9:08					
	9:16					80, 90
Get papers for meet.	9:16 9:24					
Men's room						
Budget meeting	9:30					
	11:52					70—Quality Make up charts Automatic deposit
Bank— cash check	12:02 12:22					
Helms	12:23					
	12:26	Tell Ellie	2	0		
	12:28	Tell Sy	6	50	2	
Lunch	12:52	with Helms				
Men's room						
Return	2:01					
Helms	2:06					
	2:09	Sec.— Typing	8	25%	2	
	2:22	Telephone	5	0%	—	
	3:04	Secretary	5	0%	0	
	3:16	Sent Helms for documen- tation				
	3:24	Helms back				
	3:26	Sent again	16	100%		
	3:29	returned				
	4:06					
Calls	4:12 4:27					
Sec.	4:28					
Dic- tate	5:06					
	5:09	Disturbed by people passing by				
	5:15	Harry				
	5:43	Mind drift	7	100	3	
	6:27					

himself any quantity grade, probably because he couldn't control what went on at the meeting, and he notes "Make up charts." When I questioned him two or three weeks later, he said he decided to make up charts for the next meeting, in order to make his explanations clearer. He had very sound reasons for doing this. He indicated that after this meeting he started using charts at all meetings with nontechnical people, and that it helped him enormously. This little comment, in his opinion, changed his effectiveness in a very substantial way.

His next notation is at 12:02, "Bank cash check," to 12:22 and another interesting comment: "Automatic deposit." He decided that, since he was spending that much time, he would use the automatic deposit system. At 12:23, "Helms": I'm not sure whether he called Helms at the time, or brought him in; he didn't remember. At 12:26, "Tell Ellie." At 12:28, "Tell Sy." He apparently had given instructions to people. At 12:52, lunch with Helms. You'll notice that at 2:06 Helms arrives at his office and remains for most of the rest of the day. The manager was doing an appraisal of Helms's work, and trying to give him concrete advice on how he could improve. The chart doesn't indicate this, because he didn't think it was necessary to write it down. He said that he decided then that Helms and every other engineer would have to come to the meetings better prepared, which would help them get through those meetings much more effectively. The reason he pointed that out is that at 3:16 he sent Helms back to get more documentation, and he wasted fifteen or sixteen minutes. This work-flow chart, although it is far less complete than the attorney's, apparently was far more effective in the long run. Only three months after doing his first work-flow chart, this managing engineer was told by his supervisor that he was performing at a much higher level, and was being considered for one of the top posts in his firm. He attributes his tremendous increase in efficiency to this system. He did agree that a more detailed work-flow chart would be more useful, and that he would be more detailed in his updated chart.

The fourth personal productivity chart (see page 80 –81) is one I filled in myself. It is a traveling chart. I decided that since I spend a good deal of my time on the road, and work when I travel, I should run a work chart on that time. This was a typical chart. I left the house at 7:02, arrived at La Guardia Airport at 8:06, boarded the plane at 8:30, and took off at 8:50. At 9:01 I started preparing my presentation, and I worked from 9:15 until 10:43, when I prepared for landing. I noted two interruptions, one from a stewardess, one from mind drift and one from a trip to the lavatory. I graded myself 95 and 95. I found my driver, arrived at the hotel, went to my room, made several calls, lay down, called the desk for a wake-up call, dressed, found the host, checked the room and spoke at 3:30. Finished at 5:16 and left for the airport at 5:45. Arrived at 6:10, took off at 6:25, read a magazine until 7:20. At 7:20 I started working on a speech for the next day, and I worked until 8:13. During that time my mind drifted off three times. My comment made the entire chart worthwhile. I gave myself only 50 and 50 as marks; my quality and quantity weren't satisfactory, and my comment was "Do over." As a result of this chart and several more like it, I changed the time I worked on my speeches: I now work in the morning when flying to a speech and relax on the way home.

This chart demonstrates how even a very sketchy chart can point out a major work flaw.

Job	Time	Source of Interruption	Time Wasted	% My Fault	Additional Time Wasted	Comments, Quality & Quantity Score
Left house	7:02					
Airport	8:06					
Board	8:30					
Takeoff	8:50					
Write report	9:01					
	9:02	Mind drift	2	100		
	9:06	Coffee	1	100		
	9:11	Lav.	3	0		
	9:15					95, 95
	10:18					
	10:19					
	10:32					95, 95
	10:32					
Prepare for landing	10:43					
Arrived	10:58					
Find driver	11:30					
Arrived hotel	12:15					
Arrive room	12:32					
Call 1	12:34					
2	12:50					
3	12:53					
4	1:12					
Call desk for wake-up call	1:25					
Up	2:20					
Toilet and dress	2:35					
	2:43					
Call clients Call 1	2:43					
2	2:46					
3	2:56					
4	3:07					
5	3:16					
Speech	3:30					
	5:16					

Job	Time	Source of Interruption	Time Wasted	% My Fault	Additional Time Wasted	Comments, Quality & Quantity Score
Left for airport	5:45					
Arrival	6:10					
Took off	6:25					
Read magazine	6:25					
	7:20					
Worked on speech	7:20					
	7:24	Mind drift	3	100%	2	
	7:36	Mind drift	1	100%	1	
	7:42	Mind drift	6	100%	0	
	7:53	Goof off	2	100%	0	
	7:59					
	8:06					25, 25
	8:13					(First score— then reconsidered because it was too low)
	8:25					50, 50
Arrive home	10:02					Ineffective at end of day—don't write speeches then. DO OVER

CHAPTER SIX

Organization

I Needed Help

The only item on my desk other than a pen holder and a plaque is the yellow sheet of paper on which I am writing. For the first time in years, my desk and my work area are immaculate. Usually both are piled with papers. In the past I maintained that I knew where every paper was and that it didn't slow me down to have them piled on and around my desk, but the fact was that I was lying, not to the world, but to myself. It did slow me down. I spent time looking for pens and papers, and hunting through my files to find this fact or that statistic; and for a researcher, this is very time-consuming and counterproductive. On occasion, searching for one fact or one statistic took so long it broke my train of thought and set me back not minutes but hours or days. Nevertheless, I maintained that fiction, because like most human beings I hate to admit I'm flawed.

Not wanting to admit you're flawed is a universal characteristic. Most of us rationalize away our bad habits and still manage to do our work with a certain amount of skill and precision. However, for a researcher that flaw can be—and was for me—almost deadly. My experience as a researcher showed me that, if before a researcher started a study he believed he knew the results, he would be very likely to take his beliefs and superimpose them on the research, and the final results would reflect his prejudice rather than reality. Unfortunately, when I started researching Organization, that is exactly what I did.

Since I did not keep my personal work area neat, I rationalized that being neat wasn't really that important. My reasoning ran that as long as I wasn't Oscar in *The Odd Couple*, I was okay. My desk wasn't that bad. The fact that stacks of papers were piled on top most of the time really didn't make that much difference. I was always able to find what I needed. I might have to shuffle through a few papers, but how long could that take? In fact, I actually believed that having stacks of papers within reach was a form of organization. I convinced myself that, since I instantly could lay my hands on the statistics I was using, this disorder actually added to my efficiency.

My argument with myself ran something like this: I did plan everything; as a researcher you must. With a desk piled with papers, I had written computer programs to choose men's and women's clothing with over six million variables, without owning a computer. I had taken very complicated research and turned it into a readable book, while writing a column and running three separate companies. I was able to do all this because I have the ability to hold a great number of ideas in my mind simultaneously, and this ability made me an organized person. This, of course, is not true. The fact is that my intelligence allowed me to succeed in spite of being disorganized.

I didn't accept the fact that having a disorganized environment made me less effective, even after I interviewed dozens of executives, all of whom maintained that people with disorganized environments were ineffective. Fortunately, I built into my research a system of checks, because, although I'm not always a realist, I'm a good researcher. The first rule in my organization is that after a research project has been completed, which means the data have been collected and analyzed, the raw data are given to a second party for independent review and analysis. Whether I manage a research project personally or it's run by one of my staff, the rule applies. I was so sure that my analysis of these interviews about disorganized environments was accurate that I made sure that the research was reviewed by three of my best people, who were very well organized.

To my surprise and dismay, after they reviewed the data the conclusions they drew were dramatically different from mine. I can summarize their findings in one sentence. They said that neatness counts: if a person is not neat, he is not organized, and if he's not organized, he's not nearly as efficient as he could be.

When I read their report, I wasn't very upset because I didn't think it was accurate. I immediately challenged them to prove their statements. Since my challenge was personal, they returned the challenge. They said that if I put my work area in order, I would be more efficient, and they would prove it. They started by doing a time and motion study on my daily activities. They included writing my column, drawing up reports, answering the phone, returning calls, making appointments, conducting consultations, preparing speeches. They limited their studies to these activities because these were the activities I conducted in the research office. They then, with my help, organized my work area. Everything was assigned to and put in its place, and under their watchful eyes I put everything away when I finished using it. Through their efforts, my desk, which was usually piled high with papers, was neat and clean. Then they did a second time and motion study. The results surprised no one but me, and I frankly was astounded. I was far more efficient in my new orderly environment. I completed all the measured jobs in less time.

There was no question that organizing my desk and my work environment dramatically increased my productivity without my making any additional changes in work style.

Myths About Organization

While destroying my personal myth, they also destroyed one of the great myths about organization, that is, that someone else can organize you. I've had good secretaries and efficient assistants for years, and many of them have attempted to organize me. However, since people working for me don't have as much understanding of my research as I do, there was no way they could succeed without my assistance. They didn't know which papers were important or which ones I was going to use that day or which ones I didn't need at all. If I told them to leave a pile of papers lying in the corner of my desk, they left it, because I was the boss and I believed I needed the information at my fingertips at that moment. In a sense I was often right. When I kept research statistics on my desk, I wasn't making a silly mistake. Having the information at my fingertips often helped me handle difficult projects. However, after I piled twenty or thirty stacks of papers on my desk, it overwhelmed me. There's a point at which piling things on your desk becomes counterproductive. Only after my assistants forced me to organize myself did I understand this.

One of the problems with other people organizing you is that they have to know as much about your job as you do, and they have to have work styles identical to yours. Therefore, in reality, the only person who can organize you is you. Which means most of the books about organization are meaningless, because the authors want to run your life. The myth on which the majority of these books are based is that disorganized people do not know how to organize—and that's nonsense. When we asked poorly organized people to draw up plans for organizing themselves, they did as well as most of the authors. Housewives really don't need anyone to tell them where their suits and shirts should go, and business people can certainly put papers in file drawers and cross-reference them. Being able to count and knowing the alphabet are really all that is required. The fact is that in 90 percent of the cases, being disorganized has nothing to do with not knowing how to organize. In most cases, being disorganized is nothing more than having developed a series of bad habits. One disorganized person after another told us he knew that when he finished with papers he should put them in his files. People understood that their closets and desks should be in order. They were fully aware of the fact that they should be neater. What they didn't have was the neatness habit. Which means if you're disorganized and wish to become organized, all you have to develop is a new set of habits. You have to recondition yourself, and get yourself into the habit of doing these things that will make you into an organized person. It sounds simple, and it is.

Once I discovered that, the next step was obvious. I set out to identify which habits make a person organized. When I first started questioning people who were organized about why they were organized, they gave me so many different answers that they confused the issue. Everyone seemed to have a different definition of organization. Some differences could be traced to job training, age, background, and personality, but there didn't seem to be any overall pattern. The pattern developed only after we interviewed more than four hundred people. We concluded that there were four elements to organization: a sense of place, a sense of time, a sense of order, and a sense of priority. Although all these are related, it is possible to have one characteristic without having the others, and most people have strong and weak points. Those with a sense of place are people who put everything away. They're neat, they keep their papers in files, and they know where their pencils, their pads, their bank books are. They're people with neat desks. People who have a sense of order know in which order they're going to attack things. They know which things come first, second, and third. The minute they approach a problem, they arrange it in some sort of order. People with a sense of time know when they're going to complete various projects. They have a sense of when they'll finish the first part of a project, the second part, the third part, and the final part, and they usually stick to a schedule. Finally, people with a sense of priority immediately decide how important anything is, and which things take precedence over others.

Organization of Place

I will start by discussing organization of place, because I lack the skill myself, and because it is the weakness that is most likely to sink your career. I only became aware of this several months ago while doing an image survey at a client's headquarters. When I arrived I found several corporate officers, including the president, waiting for me. They said that they wanted to go through headquarters with me to get my immediate reaction to each department. Since they were paying for the research, I saw no reason why they shouldn't.

As we proceeded from one department to another, I made my comments, and asked them for theirs. Being a research opportunist, I realized I had a golden opportunity. As the morning drew on, I could see that we agreed about most things. The only difference was that they were incensed when they ran across individuals hidden from public view whose personal environments were disorganized. People with papers piled high on their desk or who were disheveled enraged them. In fact, the president asked me why I didn't draw attention to these people. I said that my job there was to handle only those people who had public contact, and most of the disheveled people didn't. In the early afternoon we ran across a young man whose desk was so messy that the president dressed him down publicly. When he finished he asked an assistant to make up a list of the messy people we ran across, because he wanted to send each of them a memo. He said he had another reason for wanting to know who they were. Even if they straightened their desks, he would never trust one of them with an important assignment. The other executives all agreed.

When I left that day I wondered whether the other executives were being yes-men when they agreed with the president, or whether they really believed that anyone whose work area was disheveled couldn't be trusted. So I conducted a small survey of fifty-two executives. I asked them what their reactions were to people whose personal areas were constantly in a state of disarray. Fifty of the fifty-two said that they were totally turned off by anyone who had his desk piled high with papers and they agreed with the president of the company I just left—they wouldn't trust a person like that with an important assignment. In addition, thirty-six made the unsolicited comment that they would not want to be personally associated with that type of person. Which means that if you look disheveled, you don't have the chance of a proverbial snowball in Haiti of moving up in corporate America. You can't be a winner if the winners will not work with you.

If you're not in the habit of organizing your personal area, there's a very simple rule that will help, which we discovered after interviewing several dozen people who had learned to keep their work areas neat. The rule is when you're not using it, put it away. To be more specific: if you're not going to use it in the next two hours, put it away. If you're not going to use papers on your desk immediately, put them in your desk or in your file or wherever they belong, and do this right away. If you have no place for an item, make one. If you're not using a pen or pencil, put it in your drawer or your pocket. If your telephone book is not being used, close it and put it away. At the end of every job, clean your desk. Don't go to lunch unless your desk is clean. At the end of the day the same rule applies. If you're sloppy, at first you're going to find this very annoying and all this activity may seem counterproductive. You'll spend so much time putting things away and taking them out that you'll really wonder if you're wasting your time. You won't be. If you continue to obey this simple "put it away rule" for six weeks, you'll start developing the habit of neatness. If you put everything in its place as soon as you finish using it, your work area will be neater and you will be better organized and more efficient.

If you start slipping, one of the best tricks to help you get back on track is to walk away from your desk, look at it, and ask yourself what kind of a person works in that area. One gentleman we spoke to said that this cured him instantly. He said that one day he was walking through his office and looked over another man's desk and said to himself, "What a slob." It was only after he made this comment that he realized the other man was no sloppier than he, and he assumed that if he judged the other man this way, everyone was saying the same thing about him. He went back to his desk and immediately cleaned it up. We found when we interviewed executives that many believed that people's personal environments were extensions of their personality. The minute I became aware of this, I became very uncomfortable having a desk that was totally disheveled. In fact, anytime my desk becomes a little bit disheveled, I stand back and ask myself what kind of a person works there, and then I clean it up.

A Sense of Time

The second habit that everyone agrees is essential to an organized person is having a sense of time. There are people who are very neat, even precise, and they keep their work areas beautiful. Their offices look as if they were designed by Office Beautiful or Better Housekeeping. Yet these same people constantly show up late for meetings and always finish their job just before or after the deadline. It may come as a surprise to hear this if you're one of them, but you're just as disorganized as the person with the sloppy desk, particularly if your problem with time carries over into your work. Say you start an eight-hour day with eight hours of work, and because the day looks so long at nine o'clock in the morning, you work at a relaxed pace. By three in the afternoon you discover that between three and five you have to do four hours of work, so you arrange to do it. Naturally, the quality of that work is not what it should be. In fact, one of the ways of spotting whether you have this problem is to see if the quality of your work varies dramatically from job to job.

There are several steps you can take if you have a problem handling time. The first is a very simple one: get a clock. The second is equally simple: run work-flow charts on yourself and run them often. The work-flow chart which we described in an earlier chapter will allow you to see how much time you're actually spending on any job. The third step is to have an alarm wristwatch or an alarm clock that you set to go off every twenty or thirty minutes. Naturally, you can use your desk clock for this purpose, but most of our trainees preferred wrist alarms, which allowed them to continue training while away from their desks. The repeating alarm is a technique developed independently by two gentlemen who had difficulty judging time. Each said the alarm made him conscious of time. Every time it went off he asked himself what he had done for the last twenty or thirty minutes, and what he expected to do for the next twenty or thirty minutes. Both said that by constantly reminding themselves of the passage of time, it didn't slip by and they had a greater handle on it.

In addition to time as measured in minutes, you have to have a feeling for extended periods of time—days, weeks, months, years. The best way to develop this sense is to keep a daily calendar and to list each job as you start it and mark it when you intend to finish. Then indicate on the calendar how you expect the job to progress. This will force you to stick to a schedule and give you a sense of extended time.

Deadlineitis

One of the worst results of a poor sense of time is deadlineitis. If you're a person who always completes projects at the last minute, you have this very deadly productivity disease. Most people who have deadlineitis believe that the quantity of work they finish is their main problem. In actual fact it isn't; the most serious problem is the quality of work. We found that workers who finished their assignments just before they were due often handed them in whether they were ready or not. They hardly ever reviewed their work and did that necessary upgrading which is the final step of most jobs. Once they overcame this problem, they dramatically improved the quality of their work.

But improving work quality is not the only reason for working on the problem. We found that the majority of the people with deadlineitis were not only late with their projects, they were late for appointments as well, and were not late because they were inconsiderate, or even because they didn't plan their time. They were late because they didn't think in terms of time. When they had a ten o'clock appointment, they would start shutting down their job at five to ten. They never allowed themselves five minutes to walk to the other end of the building or five minutes to get their papers together, or a few more minutes to go to the men's or ladies' room. As a result, they always drifted into meetings late. And they were not just late for meetings, they were late for everything. They didn't plan to be late, it was just the way things seemed to happen. It wasn't that they didn't know it would take a few minutes to put their papers away, they were just not in the habit of thinking in those terms. They had sloppy habits of thinking. When a project was due on Wednesday, they would invariably plan to have it ready Tuesday night. If anything interfered with their schedule, and something almost always does, they were late.

Of course, in any organization, particularly large ones, this is a deadly flaw. The reason it's so deadly is that organizations are just that—they are groups of interdependent people. If the boss calls a meeting for twelve people and each person is to bring a certain amount of information and one person doesn't show up on time, not only is the boss wasting his time, the missing person is wasting the time of the eleven other people, and this is something that no executive can, will, or should tolerate. As a result, people who are constantly late find themselves shoved into very unimportant dead-end jobs, because not being reliable is the first and most deadly sin in any organization.

I didn't come up with a solution to this problem; a manager in a Fortune 500 company did. He said that he had two men working for him, both of whom were excellent workers and produced high-quality work if he handled them correctly. When he started working with them, he noticed they were both constantly late. His solution was that when he needed something Tuesday, he insisted they have it on his desk Monday, and then if they didn't, he raised Cain with them. In addition, after the assignment was handed in Monday, if it needed extra work, he often gave it back and insisted they correct it right away. In this way, he got top-notch work from two people who would normally give him second-rate material. He made the same adjustment for meetings. He insisted that when there's a meeting at ten o'clock, they be in front of his door at five to ten.

If you have the problem of deadlineitis, you can solve it in the same way. The trick is to plan to finish every assignment ahead of time. If you have a meeting at ten o'clock, be ready to go to that meeting at nine-thirty. You needn't leave your desk until five to ten if it's a five-minute walk, but have everything you need for that meeting ready by then. You can use a checklist, allowing time to go to the men's or ladies' room, and time to get the papers together. In addition, if you have a job that is due by Friday, finish that job on Thursday. If you must, build in a reward and punishment system for finishing on schedule. If you finish on Thursday instead of Friday, you can then go back and look at your job and see if you wish to do something to improve it, but don't count on that time. Have the job completed and ready to hand in Thursday. We found that this simple technique created a different set of work habits and made life easier and more productive for the people who adopted it.

The Habit of Planning

The most important organizational habit is the habit of planning. It touches on all the other areas, but it is separate. When we talk about planning, we're talking about lining up all the steps in a job. We found that effective workers plan a job and ineffective ones do not. Many of them claim to, but if you stopped them in the middle of a job and asked them what are the next three steps or when they expected to be at point one, two, or three, they wouldn't have an answer. When we asked effective people the same questions, they usually rattled off when they expected to finish various stages of a job, and in which order they were going to handle them. Some would do this verbally, and others would draw a very complex plan from their desk. But they all had a plan.

In addition, our interviews with effective and ineffective workers indicated that effective workers had a planning habit. They planned everything. When we asked effective workers what they intended to be doing in three years or five years or ten years, in six out of ten cases they were able to give a definite answer. In about 20 percent of the cases, although they had no definite plan, they had what we considered a pretty good idea of where they wanted to be. Only 20 percent of them really didn't seem to have any plan at all. When we interviewed ineffective workers, the statistics almost stood on their head. Approximately 60 percent of them had no idea what they were going to be doing, 25 percent had some idea, and only 15 percent had a definite plan. Apparently planning is a habit, and people who plan their lives are more likely to plan their daily work and to be more effective as a result.

Setting Goals

If you're one of those people who do not have long-term goals, it is essential that you set them. Having long-term goals will automatically put you in a planning mode. In addition, long-term goals can have effects on your daily activities that in some ways are greater than those of short-term goals. Worthwhile long-term goals, such as making a million dollars, making your family secure, becoming an attorney, becoming a doctor, can give one a sense of mission.

You must choose a long-term goal, and you must commit to that goal in writing. You can choose any goal, even if you never expect to achieve it, as long as you commit yourself to trying and the goal is not silly. It would be silly if John T. Molloy at age forty-seven wanted to be a football player. It would be equally silly if John T. Molloy at age forty-seven said he wanted to be a general. Chances of becoming a general, if you're not in the military, are extremely remote at best. However, if I set my goal to be elected governor of a state or to be elected to some other major office, although it's not an ambition I would find easy to achieve, it's one that I could achieve in my lifetime, and therefore it's an acceptable goal because it is at least doable in theory.

The reason we ask you to find a goal is that, until you do, your life and your work and everything around you will drift. We discovered this when we questioned people without goals. They find that they can't work hard at anything because nothing is that important. Therefore, when you choose a goal, you should attribute importance to it —which means that you have to have a goal that has an emotional value for you. This will enable you to develop a sense of mission. The reason it's so important to develop this sense of mission is that a number of studies have found that men and women with a sense of mission perform at a high level, no matter what they're doing. A classic example is the people involved in the moon shot. There were several studies on the effectiveness of workers in the aerospace industry before, during, and after the moon shot. All these studies showed that average employees performed at a much higher level when they were working on the moon shot. They did so because they felt a sense of mission. One can find the same sense of mission during wars or crises. The statement that there are no great men, just great challenges, is in a sense true. In spite of that, you can be great, can have a sense of mission, even if your job is not sending an astronaut to the moon or saving democracy. If you can identify a worthwhile long-term goal and develop an emotional attachment to it, you will automatically become more productive.

If the reason escapes you, consider a high-school student who sets her goal to be President of the United States. If that high-school student can fall in love with that goal, make it her mission, she will be forced to start doing things that day that will help her move toward her goal. She is going to start asking herself some very tough questions. The first and most obvious is what must a woman do to become President of the United States. If she looks at it logically, she'll see that most Presidents are politicians from major states. Since before becoming politicians most persons become attorneys, she's probably going to have to become an attorney. As a high-school student, she would then have to reason that in order to attend law school, she would have to have excellent grades in college, and it would help if she went to a good college. It's obvious that to gain admission to a good college, she's going to have to have good grades in high school. If she's a sophomore and doing C and D work, she's going to have to adjust her life-style to suit her long-term goals. Otherwise she does not have goals, just daydreams.

Her first step would be to look at the subjects she's taking, and see if there is any way in which she can get A's immediately. Let us assume that she's a bright student with a gift for math and science, and she's taking physics and algebra. She can almost guarantee herself A's or at least very high grades by working hard in those subjects. If in addition to those two subjects she's taking social studies and history, she can again guarantee herself good grades in those areas through simple effort, because most of the information required on tests is a product of memory and memory is a product of effort. If she spends enough time with her history and social studies books, she will know the answers that are required to get good grades. And finally, if she's taking a creative-writing course, she's going to have to develop an entire set of skills to get a higher grade. She cannot guarantee that she'll improve her writing skills overnight; she cannot simply cram for a writing course. She's going to have to start reading more. She's probably going to ask the teacher for extra assignments, and it would be a good move to ask the teacher if she might look at an A composition, if she's never written one, so that she can see what an A composition looks like, feels like, and sounds like. There are all sorts of realistic steps this young woman is going to have to take today, and if she has a real sense of mission, she'll take them.

One of the questions that always crops up at this point, particularly when I talk to young people, and I talk to them all the time, is how can I choose a goal. How can I develop a sense of mission. This generation is a generation without heroes. The only public figures that are held up as idols for our young people these days are rock stars, movie stars, and athletes, all of whom seem to go out of their way to set bad examples.

When I interviewed two thousand successful men and women for my *Live for Success* book, I found that one of the characteristics many had in common was that early in their youth they became infatuated with a historical figure. The involvement usually began when they were forced or cajoled into reading a biography or autobiography. Reading about the great man or the great woman was so moving that they aspired to become like that person. This is one of the finest sources of motivation in the world, and that is why I suggest that young people read the biographies of people they like and admire. If they read enough of them, they will sooner or later find a hero or heroine worth following, an idol who will give them a sense of mission.

For most of us, if we think about it, long-range goals are rather easy to pick. You want to make X number of dollars a year, become president or vice president of a company, a partner in a firm, to double your business, and so on. Picking the goal is simple. Determining what steps are necessary to attain the goal may take a bit more thought, but it's absolutely necessary. In fact, it's necessary to commit to those steps in writing. It is very important to say exactly what you're going to have to do to reach your goal, because unless you're committed to each and every step, you're not committed to the goal itself. A goal is something from which you have a step-by-step series of challenges. Each challenge will have an importance of its own, and importance will be added to it because the challenge will be looked upon as a critical step toward your final goal. Each time you're challenged, you'll start thinking of the steps necessary to overcome your challenge, and this automatically will lead you into the habit of planning.

If you do not at present have the habit of planning, it's a very simple habit to develop. Every time you undertake a new job, take out a piece of paper and write down the steps necessary to finish that job and the order in which you expect to do them. The first step in planning is listing.

Second, after you've listed all the steps, look for the pitfalls. If your report is due in two weeks, and it requires that you read nine separate documents, make a trip to the library, and interview two people, you can look at each step and decide in which order they should be completed. If you find that the nine documents are available, decide in which order you're going to read them; then decide which of the two people is the easier to interview, and whether you should do the interviews before or after you do part or all of the reading. If one of the people is known to be hard to get to, if he's the type of person who always makes a big deal giving you fifteen minutes of his time, make an appointment for next Tuesday knowing you'll have all the preliminary work done by then to make the interview go well. Obviously we're in an area where time and order become entwined, but don't let that bother you. You're still basically thinking of putting things in order.

Once you've worked out several plans, planning will become an essential part of your life. Planning is nothing more than making life simpler. For those who plan all the time, writing down the steps for each job will seem silly at first. For those who don't plan, the process will seem like a waste of time. Both groups must force themselves. After two or three months you can stop writing down the steps for those jobs that have become rote, because by the third month planning simple jobs will become a habit and you'll do it automatically. But you will have to continue to plan more complex jobs on paper. If you're over thirty-five and you're in the habit of planning, however, you may be able to skip making detailed plans even on large jobs. Cryptic notes will do as well, but put something in writing. The key is to commit your plan of progress to writing, and then check back and see how carefully you stuck to it, and where you've gone wrong.

Setting Priorities: A Woman's Problem

Most people we spoke to thought that women were better organized than men. Women are less likely to show up late for meetings or hand in work late. They are more likely to create written plans before they act, and they are a lot neater than men. However, many women have one critical flaw: they are very poor at setting priorities. It is this element of organization that gets them into the most trouble. It's the main stumbling block for most women headed for the executive suite. We interviewed twenty-six women executives who had a number of women working for them, and each of them said that the main problem for the women under them is that they get bogged down in details. They are trapped by a particularly feminine sense of organization. They almost seem to have blinders on, and don't take into consideration the things going on around them. They see a goal, they know where they're going, they plan the steps to get there, and then they simply go for it. It's very admirable, but it doesn't work in a fluid environment.

With the help of several women executives, I came up with a series of questions that every woman should ask about every job she undertakes. She should ask, first, what is the final object of the job; second, what is the end product; third, how this job is going to affect her, her boss, the department, the company; and fourth, has anything changed in her environment, her boss's environment, the department environment, or the company environment that should cause her to reassess what she's doing. Instead of discussing the problem, which didn't work in the past, we typed the questions on a small sheet of paper and gave it to a dozen women who had been identified as having a problem with priorities. We asked them to ask themselves these questions every day. At the end of three months we went back and asked their bosses, who had identified them as being too narrow, how they were doing. In eight out of twelve cases, the boss indicated that the woman had improved dramatically, that she was now taking a broad-brush approach to problems, and that she had substantially increased her chance of moving up in the company.

The one thing that both male and female executives agreed on was that, although this last flaw was usually found in women, it was also found in men. There are many men who fail because they have no sense of priorities, and if you're one of those men, the same steps that saved the women can save you.

The Bismarck Factor

I thought that I had finished this chapter until I asked several dozen male and female executives in large corporations and several dozen successful self-employed people what they thought of it. Their answer was that it was good as far as it went, but it didn't go far enough. Most of them agreed I missed an essential element: I call it the Bismarck factor.

The Iron Chancellor was said always to have had a second plan sitting in his drawer. He was supposed to have had plans to cover every contingency. No matter what happened, he was ready. These very successful men and women said that, if you're truly organized, this type of planning is essential. An organized person is someone who can walk into a disorganized environment and bring a sense of order to it. They pointed out that top executives often become top executives by taking over departments or companies that are running downhill, and bringing them back. People at the top often get there by being troubleshooters—they go in where everything is going wrong and make it right. These very successful people indicated that organization is not only within the individual, but within the environment and within the job. Every job and every environment requires its own form of organization, and a truly organized person is adaptable, and ready for all eventualities.

They went on to say that when a top executive takes over any project, not only does that executive have a plan for the job, he has either in writing or in the back of his mind several plans to cover contingencies. In addition, he uses the organizational abilities of the people around him to help keep him organized. He recognizes people's organizational strong points—and their shortfalls. He demands that others fit into his sense of organization and help him obtain his goal. He surrounds himself only with people who can adjust to his way of doing things or his sense of organization, which makes flexibility a critical element of organization, particularly for men and women who are working their way up in an organization. As one executive put it, there are only two types of people working for him: the organized and efficient, and the disorganized and inefficient.

If you want to be one of the organized and efficient, follow the advice in this chapter.

CHAPTER SEVEN

Concentration, Focusing, Goofing Off and Goldbricking

Concentration and Focusing

Observations of good and poor workers and our interviews with them and their superiors have led us to one inescapable conclusion: the ability to concentrate and/or focus is central to productivity. In every case where we were able to increase a person's ability to concentrate or focus, we improved his productivity.

When I first started working with my employees to increase their productivity, naturally I attempted to increase their ability to concentrate. The minute I started measuring their ability to concentrate, it became evident that I had to make two measurements—one, the ability to concentrate, and the other the ability to focus—because, although they were related, they were obviously separate skills. In our studies we define concentration as the ability to stick with the task without interruption, while we define focus as the ability to stick with a project in spite of interruptions. This means that if you start working at nine o'clock and at 9:02 the best-looking man or woman in your office walks past your desk and you stare at him or her, you've broken concentration. If you immediately put that person out of your mind and go back to work without undue interruption, you have not broken focus. If two minutes later you start thinking about a dance you'll be attending that night, you've once again broken concentration, but if you put that thought out of your mind almost immediately, you have maintained focus. It is not unusual for conscientious workers to have their concentration broken a half a dozen or dozen times in an hour without their pausing for a significant period, which means that, although their concentration is broken time and again, they continue to maintain their focus and continue to work effectively. If, however, twenty-five minutes later that same beautiful person walks by once more and this time you not only glance at the person but start daydreaming about being trapped on a desert island with him or her, you've broken focus. The difference between breaking concentration and breaking focus is qualitative and quantitative: quantitative because the break in focus takes more time and qualitative because it takes a restarting effort to get back into the job. In fact, if there is one way of separating the two when you're not sure, ask yourself if the break in activity requires a restarting effort. If it does, you've broken focus.

Goofing Off and Goldbricking

Of course, as the title indicates, I recognize two other causes of diminished productivity, goofing off and goldbricking. The difference between breaking focus and goofing off is both quantitative and qualitative. If you break focus, you start thinking of yourself on a desert island with that wonderful person. However, this is an unconscious act, it's not a planned one. The minute you become conscious that you've interrupted your work with this fantasy, and decide to lean back in your chair, put your feet on your desk, and spend time thinking of that desert island and that wonderful dalliance, you're goofing off. Of course, goofing off can include, and often does include, more than mental dalliance. It can include trips to the water fountain, the men's room, the ladies' room, stepping out for a drink in the afternoon, visiting your local movie theater. You're goofing off at any time that you're consciously stopping work when you should be working.

Before going any further, I will admit that I occasionally goof off. I've been known to put on my bathing suit in the middle of a hot, sunny afternoon and go down and take a dip in the pool, when I should be back at the office working, but goofing off is not a problem for me since I do it very rarely. It only becomes a problem when it interferes with your ability to be productive in a major way, and it becomes even a more serious problem when you can't control it. I assumed when I started researching this book that if someone was goofing off, all he really had to do was make up his mind to stop, and he could. However, after interviewing several hundred people who were identified as goof-offs, I became aware that they fell into two categories. The first group of people goofed off occasionally, and did it consciously. The second group couldn't help goofing off, and I dubbed them goldbricks. They believe that they're taking a conscious break in work, but they're really not. Goofing off for them is a habit they can't break. In fact, it's an addiction for some, and in order to cure it they have to recognize it as an addiction and treat it as one.

I know that many of the best workers reading this book are finding this statement ridiculous. In fact, they may be enraged by it. They may think I'm giving people an excuse to goof off, but I'm really not. Most of the people who run America are effective workers, and because they've always been effective workers, they don't understand ineffective ones. They're in the same position when talking about goldbricking as nonsmokers are when they talk about smoking. Nonsmokers often say, "I don't know why people have a filthy habit like that." They don't understand it because they've never had an addiction similar to it; and it is this lack of understanding on the part of good workers, who are usually the people in positions of authority, that stops them from helping the goldbricks in this world, who are one of the major productivity problems in our society. In fact, people with the habit of goldbricking have become a large segment of the American work force. There are literally millions of American workers who couldn't do a day's work if they wanted to.

Contrary to the opinion expressed by many of the managers we interviewed, the minute I explain to people that goldbricking is an addiction, they do not jump up and admit they are addicted. In fact, it's the hardest thing in the world to get people to admit even to themselves, and therefore we discovered a very simple way for people to identify whether they're goldbricking or goofing off. You're a goldbrick if you spend a good part of your day goofing off without realizing where the day went. If you're not sure how often you do this, there's a very simple test you can take. Take out your daily calendar and set aside as many as half a dozen times during the day when you're going to goof off. Mark them on your calendar, being very specific: set aside ten minutes between two and three to go to the water fountain, ten minutes between three and four to go to the men's room, fifteen minutes to have a drink in the afternoon, and so on. If you're a goof-off and all it takes is a conscious effort for you to break the habit, you'll maintain good work patterns for the rest of the day. If, however, you've become addicted to goofing off and it has become an essential part of your work style, you'll find that you do as much goofing off in the remaining time as you ever did. If you've taken this test and failed it, don't try to rationalize away the results. Recognition of the fact that goofing off has become a part of your work system is the only thing that will enable you to change.

Change is necessary whether you're a goof-off or a goldbrick, and in order to change you're going to have to make a total commitment to change. It's not going to be easy. In fact, for many it's going to be very difficult. It's not going to be something you'll accomplish in weeks; it may take months, and possibly even years. But no matter how poor a worker you are at present, you can with effort learn to be an effective worker and enjoy it.

The Avoidance Technique

Whether you're a goldbrick or a goof-off, the first technique for change is avoidance. Avoid those situations, those places, those people that lead you into goofing off. If you take an extra fifteen minutes for lunch every time you go out with Joe, Mary, or Sam, don't go to lunch with them. If you take an extra ten minutes in the ladies' room every time you go with your best friend, don't go with her. If you find that every time you go to the files you spend ten minutes there talking to anyone who's available, try not to go to the files—send someone else. Remove the source of temptation and you remove a good part of the motivation for goofing off. As I said, it isn't going to be easy. Many people who are goof-offs also have best friends who are goof-offs, and in some cases change is going to mean severing relationships.

However, the most difficult associations to break are those that are connected with other addictions. We found that many people who were goldbricks or goof-offs had their goofing off associated with other addictions. Smokers who goofed off or goldbricked almost invariably smoked when they were goofing off. Overweight people on diets almost invariably ate chocolate or other forbidden foods, and people who had drinking problems found bars where there were none. What they did was let two bad habits reinforce each other. If you find that this is your pattern, don't try to break the two habits at the same time. Work on one at a time, and since the bad habit that you're working on is the nonproductivity habit, work on that habit first.

While the avoidance technique worked equally well for both groups, the substitution technique is particularly effective for goldbricks. If you're a goldbrick, you may find you're not able to focus on your job for more than fifteen or twenty minutes at a time. Or you may find that for two hours every afternoon you seem to get very little done without a break. For those down times, plan a task that you can perform even when you're not operating at your maximum. Have a list of calls you have to make for that day, files you have to file; set aside the time to straighten out your desk; do anything you want but don't goof off. Whatever you do, don't goldbrick, even if you have to substitute a pleasant, nonproductive activity. It is far better for you to plan to take ten minutes off for coffee and a cigarette at three o'clock and to go back to work at three-ten, than to goof off for a half hour. Not only does it save you twenty minutes, you stay in control of your day and that's one of the key elements in being productive.

The best trick, however, is to replace your nonproductive time with productive time. If your job has some elements in it that you find pleasurable, leave those aside for those times during the day when you find yourself at a productivity low. It even helps if you connect your productivity with other pleasurable activities, particularly if they're nondestructive. If you're not overweight, but you do enjoy having coffee and a Danish in the afternoon, have that coffee and Danish on the days when you have produced a predetermined amount of work; make it an incentive and a reward. Be sure not to give yourself chocolate cake if you're a dieter. The dieters we trained who tried that technique said that it didn't work, that they were always faced with the problem of whether they should be more productive or lose weight. As a result, most of them said they did neither.

Refocusing

The technique we suggest for everyone is the refocusing technique. This technique requires that you train yourself to say "back to work" over and over the minute you find yourself goldbricking or lost in a nonfocusing activity. The way you train yourself to do this is very simple. You place the phrase in front of you on your desk; you put it in a place where you're bound to look when you break focus. Most of us have the habit of looking up when we break our focus. The minute you see the phrase in front of you, start repeating it. Don't repeat it just once or twice or even until you go back to work. The first week or two repeat it a dozen or two dozen times. After the first two weeks, simply repeat it until you get back to work, and you will. You will find over a period of time that the phrase becomes a self-fulfilling prophecy. If nothing else, it makes you aware of what you should be doing and gives you guilt for goofing off. Although most people will tell us that guilt is not good, the people I worked with said it was only when they felt guilty about goofing off that they did anything about it.

When I started working with young people who were addicted to goofing off, they always asked the same question: how long is it going to take? My answer was always the same: I don't know. Some of my subjects completely conquered the habit of goofing off or goldbricking in two or three weeks, and began working effectively most of the time. With others it took months, and there were a few for whom training didn't seem to work, but they represented less than 10 percent of those who tried, and I wonder how hard they tried, because I could only measure their progress, not their effort. As I said before, I believe that anyone, no matter how ineffective he is, who puts effort into it can become productive. Once you've stopped goldbricking, which means you're only goofing off every once in a while, as we all do, you can then start working on the ability to concentrate and focus. Since you can't lose focus until you break concentration, concentration is the more basic of the two skills. Therefore, you should start by training yourself to concentrate more effectively.

Measuring Your Concentration

The most sophisticated task we're going to ask you to undertake is to measure your concentration. We experimented with several techniques, and the one that worked best for most people was our first and simplest one. We gave everyone a stopwatch and told them to hit it when they started working, and hit it again when they stopped. Put the stopwatch on your desk within easy reach. If you work away from your desk, you can hang it on your belt or around your neck; it doesn't make any difference as long as it's readily available. Pick up the watch, put it in your hand, and start working. Once you find yourself getting into your work, press the button and put the watch down. The first half-dozen times you do this, you're going to find that pressing the button itself will form an interruption. Don't be upset: once you perform the task a dozen or two dozen times, it becomes so natural that you won't notice it. You'll find yourself doing it almost without thinking.

Learning to start the watch is not very tricky, but conditioning yourself to stop it as soon as something interrupts you is. The problem with hitting a stopwatch as soon as you're interrupted is that if you're interrupted by a thought and the thought comes with any force, it's likely to capture your mind and, as a result, you'll forget to press the watch. After working with scores of people, we found that after you've been measuring your concentration for a month or two, you'll press the watch most of the time, even when a thought comes on very forcefully. Which means that you will not always press the watch at the exact moment you're interrupted, but shortly afterwards, and this will leave you a number of educated guesses instead of accurate measurements. Don't worry about this. Educated guesses work. We found that if you make enough of them, you'll get a very clear idea of your ability to concentrate. Which will give you a set of measurements that will allow you to form a base from which you can start improving.

If you're starting to measure your ability to concentrate, you must understand that this ability will vary dramatically depending on a number of factors: whether you like or dislike the project, your state of mind, if you're worried or upset about something, how well you feel that day, or even if you're having an off day. In addition, familiarity with the subject will make concentration easier. Our research indicates that it is far more difficult to concentrate on a subject when it's first introduced. We also discovered that concentration connected with physical activity is dramatically different from concentration connected with purely mental activity. If you're a dancer, you'll find it easier to concentrate in the beginning of your workout than you do toward the end. The reason is simple: physical fatigue makes concentration more difficult. On the other hand, if you're a physicist working on a complicated formula in its first stages, you'll find concentration is most difficult, but if you work on it for months, you'll find it becomes easier. Therefore, you must first identify at least half a dozen similar elements that require deep uninterrupted concentration. It is best if these elements are repeated daily in your work. If you don't have half a dozen projects of this nature, you can measure your ability to concentrate by measuring how effectively you concentrate on your hobby, reading a mystery novel, or any other activity. You must also keep in mind that if you choose an area that requires a set of either mental or physical skills, your mastery of those skills will be critical to your ability to concentrate. For example, we found that students with high verbal scores found it easier to concentrate on a history text, while students with high mathematical scores found it easier to concentrate on a physics text. The reasons were obvious: students with high verbal scores were able to read and comprehend the history text with greater facility than those without, while the people with good mathematical skills were able to understand the theories of physics, which were often described in mathematical terms, more easily than those who had a limited grasp of math.

Finally, we're going to have you measure two different types of concentration. The first is forced concentration. We want you to take a stopwatch and measure the amount of time that you can force yourself to concentrate on any undertaking. Then after you have developed the habit of pressing the stopwatch at the right times, which means you press the button when you start a job and you press it when you stop, start measuring your working concentration. You'll notice that the period of forced concentration will run two or three times longer than the period of working concentration. Don't let that worry you. It's normal, and be assured that improving in either area helps both areas.

Measuring Your Ability to Focus

Before working on your concentration, you should measure your ability to focus, since some of the techniques used to improve concentration also help improve focus. To measure your focus you need an alarm clock. Set it to go off every fifteen minutes for two hours, and start working. The first time the alarm goes off, simply shut it off and go back to work. The second time the alarm goes off, stop working and look at the last fifteen minutes of production. Try to reconstruct those fifteen minutes in terms of how many times you were interrupted for a significant period of time. Note if any of those interruptions broke your train of thought, and if they did, whether at that point you broke focus. You must be very honest with yourself, even ruthless. You may already consider yourself a good worker, but you are going to be unpleasantly surprised. You won't do nearly as much as you expect. Most of you will discover that you have done very well during that first fifteen-minute period; that's why we don't measure it. When you get to the second fifteen minutes, you may find you've broken focus more than once.

   It was at this point that many of our students complained they found it very difficult to decide when there was a simple break in concentration and when there was a break in focus. Here again they asked for specific numbers. They wanted to know if a break took thirty seconds, or a minute or two minutes, into which area it fell. It's very difficult to describe breaks in focus in terms of time, because there's a tremendous variation, depending on the nature of the work. If you're not sure, guess. It's not important that you be accurate every time. Remember, the only reason you're measuring your ability to concentrate or focus is to give you a baseline from which you can measure your sure but certain improvement—a measure which will also be a guess. Guesses or estimates work. Try to be as accurate as possible, but do not worry about being inaccurate. Most people guess rather well.

Before you work on your ability to concentrate or focus, you should be aware of several factors. First, the base score that you start with will probably be inaccurate because a great deal of improvement takes place the minute you begin to take measurements. Next, one of the by-products of increasing your ability to concentrate and focus is that you'll become more aware of the number of times you're interrupted. Since there's a certain amount of subjectivity and guesswork in these measurements, most people become tougher on themselves and tend to underestimate the amount of time they work without interruption. As a result, when most people start attempting to increase their ability to focus and concentrate, they don't seem to make any progress. In fact, their first scores when trying to improve in most cases turned out to be lower than their original scores. This is very misleading. In almost all cases where we had a third party measuring overall performance, the third party recorded significant increases in productivity, while the people keeping their own measurements were reporting lack of progress in both areas, and becoming discouraged by it. Please do not become discouraged. There was often a period as long as two or even three months before students agreed that their ability to concentrate and focus had dramatically improved. Everyone else looking at them noticed it immediately. If you can hang in there, most of you will see a measurable improvement within thirty to sixty days.

The final factor you have to keep in mind before you

start is that your age will have a definite effect on your ability to improve. If you're under thirty, your improvement will be almost immediate. Not long after you begin to take measurements, you'll see a significant improvement. In fact, it will come so quickly it will surprise you. If, on the other hand, you're over forty-five, you will work long and hard before you see any real improvement. But there is a compensating factor to cheer up us older guys and gals. While the young people make progress very quickly, they can lose it just as quickly. Many of the college students who were my employees lost much of their improvement over their summer vacation, which means the effects of our training on young people are very temporary unless they continue to work at it. On the other hand, I found while working with executives that, even after a hiatus of two or three months, there was virtually no loss in productivity. Once they made progress it was permanent.

Training Yourself to Concentrate

In our training we treated concentration like any other physical activity, and our training was very successful. If you want to learn to run, practice by running. If you want to learn to kick a football, practice by kicking a football. If you want to learn to lift weights, practice by lifting weights. And if you want to learn to concentrate on law or mathematics or medicine or laying bricks, you practice by concentrating on law or medicine or mathematics or laying bricks. Apparently, learning to concentrate on different areas requires a development of different mental muscles in the same way that learning to perform different physical activities requires developing different sets of physical muscles. Although lifting weights might help a runner, he's going to learn far more about running by running; and in the same way, learning to concentrate on a novel will help a person reading a law book, but learning to concentrate by reading law books will do you a lot more good if that's your job.

The next fact you must remember is that weight lifters do not start by lifting five hundred pounds. They start by lifting a smaller amount and work their way up gradually. Once you've mastered lifting forty pounds, if you're working with a coach, he'll give you forty-one, and then forty-two, forty-three, forty-four, and so on. Gradualism is the key to improvement. The same technique works when you are doing mental weight lifting. If you find you can concentrate on a subject for a minute and a half, then try for two minutes. If you can concentrate for four and a half, try for five; if you can concentrate for eight, try for nine, and so on. The trick is to work at it every day, and at planned intervals add weight.

Before deciding the increments, you have to decide on your final target and what seems reasonable. You must look at your ability to concentrate and attempt to guess how much you could improve in one month. It has to be at least a month, because it takes that long to get into practice sessions. Whenever you estimate, make that your immediate goal. Most of my students, when they started, thought that they could increase their ability to concentrate by at least 50 percent in the first month and double their ability in six months. For some the estimate was accurate, but for most it was not. Some overestimated and some underestimated. The reason there are such vast differences among the percentages of improvement is that there are differences among the needs for improvement. Some students were in excellent shape and knew how to concentrate, and for them small increases represented tremendous achievements. Others had little or no ability to concentrate, and they could make dramatic percentage increases without really becoming effective. The first group of students were like top marathon runners who practiced for six weeks, and would be very happy if they cut a minute or two off their times. The second set of students were like 350-pound out-of-shape chubbies who decide for the first time to run a marathon. In the first six weeks of exercise, those people might triple, even quadruple the distances they could run. If you're a very effective worker, I suggest that you lower your expectations, and if you're a very ineffective worker, I suggest you raise them. But neither you nor I will know what you're capable of doing until you try, and that's why this first month is an experimental month. If during this first month you come to the conclusion that your goals are unattainable and unrealistic, or that they're too easily attainable and don't represent a challenge, adjust them. But only make one adjustment during that first month, and wait at least five days to make that adjustment. Then start as if you were beginning fresh.

Since it's best if you practice concentrating in the area where you're going to be doing it most, you should try to isolate several areas of your work in which your productivity is not affected by other people, because it's very difficult to measure your productivity if it depends on the work and efficiency of others. Next, choose an area where you can measure your ability to concentrate realistically. If you're a pilot and you have to concentrate during take-offs and landings, you can't be hitting a stopwatch, because that activity could cause you to run the plane into the ground. It would be far better to practice or measure your concentration when you're doing your flight plans. Next, choose an area where improving your ability to concentrate will affect the quality of your work. This is one of the ways of giving yourself instant gratification and making improvement easier. You should also attempt to choose an area of work for which you can arrange the time and place that you work. This is particularly important, because we ask you to cut yourself off from the rest of the world when you first start practicing to improve. And finally, before you start, make sure you have a very thorough physical, and explain to the doctor that you're going to be put under tremendous physical and mental stress. I suggest furthermore that you have a doctor monitor you during your entire training period. The reason this is so important is that concentration, although it's basically a mental activity, can be physical as well. We found that when people were straining to hold a thought for an extra thirty seconds, they contorted their faces, tightened their muscles, clenched their fists, pounded the desk, and ground their teeth. One man actually crushed a glass in his hand in an effort to maintain his concentration. Since the amount of physical effort that goes into practicing concentration is enormous, I suggest that, no matter how good the physical shape you're in, you put off these exercises until the end of the day, because if you start at nine in the morning, you will find yourself exhausted by ten.

Preparing yourself to concentrate and practicing concentration is very much like preparing for and practicing lifting weights. The nature of the exercise requires that you put everything you have into it, and in order to do that effectively, you have to be in the right psychological mood. One technique suggested by several students was a relaxation technique. Before starting, they sat back in a comfortable chair, attempted to clear their mind of all other thoughts, counted to ten, or imagined a beautiful idyllic scene—one person picked a beach, another a mountain, another a blank sky—and attempted to visualize themselves in that scene being totally relaxed. After doing this, they started working. Another group said they prepared themselves by first visualizing the project—trying to see the machine they were working on or the building they were putting up, or the environments in which they were going to be working. A few visualized the project being completed, and with this end product in mind, they started. Almost everyone involved in the project said that they performed better when they were mentally prepared. We had two men who were marathoners who said that they practiced concentrating best after they ran. There was a young woman who said she exercised best in the morning, and several who said they worked best at night. It varied from individual to individual. The one thing they all agreed on is that some preparation was necessary, the preparation was essentially mental, and the process involved calming oneself down, clearing one's thoughts, forgetting the worries of the day, and getting down to the subject.

We found that you had to prepare the physical environment as well. Most prefer to concentrate in an isolated environment with low lighting. Obviously, though, if you have to read or write as part of your exercise, the lighting has to be adequate to allow you to do this comfortably. Most of the participants in these programs who could not work in a low-light environment came up with other techniques for achieving the same results. You should be seated in a comfortable chair, but not one of those luxurious chairs that many executives love. We found that people concentrated best if their desks were cleared of everything, including family pictures, and if there was nothing around them that distracted them. Sounds, sights, bright lights, noise, extraneous material had to be cut off. In addition, one man played a recording of white sound on his stereo, and another man put blinders over his glasses. All of these devices help; you have to choose the one that is most effective for you. I'm not particularly distracted by noise, but I'm very distracted by movement, so I work facing a wall. Each person has to decide which distractions bother him most.

But, like all rules, the rule to remove distractions has exceptions. While one group reported that they concentrated best after they had eliminated distractions from the environment, another used the environment in a positive way. They overwhelmed their environment with items from the job. We found that many men, in particular, kept pictures related to their work on their walls. We ran across two engineers, each of whom independently said that when he was working on a piece of equipment, it helped if the equipment was on his desk. One of them said that when he was working on a very large piece of equipment, he moved his desk down to the factory floor, so that he could look up and see it. A third engineer said he enjoyed touching the equipment as he thought about it. He closed his eyes and attempted to see the next stage in its development, and while he did that, he ran his hands over the equipment. An architect from Texas made a tape recording of the sounds of the area where he was going to put up a building, and played it over and over while he thought about the building. He said that every area had its own music, and his building had to fit into that music.

Our experience with a number of subjects indicated that a combination of these two techniques works best. Eliminating all extraneous material from the environment and bringing to the environment all those items that would help a person concentrate on the subject created an ideal situation. If a person is surrounded by a problem, and only the problem, it's very difficult for him to think of anything else but the problem for an extended period of time.

The only debate we had about concentration is whether it is transferable. About half the students believed that if you learned to concentrate on anything, you could transfer the ability, and therefore they practiced with their hobbies and in other pleasant areas. One man said he learned to concentrate only by playing chess. Another read mystery novels, and said he totally lost himself in them, and that when he brought these techniques to work, he was far more successful. On the other hand, we had students who said that there was absolutely no transfer, that they had to practice concentrating on what they were doing. There is no doubt about it—these people had greater improvement than the first group, although there was improvement among both.

As I stated earlier, there seems to be a similarity between weight lifting and learning to concentrate. In fact, concentration is really mental weight lifting, and when you start, you're going to have very stiff mental muscles. In addition, if you're out of shape, particularly for the first week or two, the amount of mental weight you'll be able to lift is going to be very small. You may even be embarrassed by it, and you may not wish to practice publicly. You should keep precise records of these early attempts, but don't pay too much attention to them. If you find you can only lift a small amount of mental weight, don't quit. The increases, when they start, will be dramatic. If you're a graduate from a typical American school, you've never been taught to concentrate. If you've never been forced to strain yourself for extended periods of time, it's going to take you at least a month to get into respectable shape so that you can perform the most basic exercises. However, once you get past this first stage of mental flabbiness, you'll be delighted, exhilarated, and uplifted by the experience —and startled at how much you've progressed.

But even those who make the greatest progress can become discouraged if they're not aware that their progress will not be steady or predictable. Progress for almost everyone is uneven and erratic. In a sense, it's like going on a diet. You reach plateaus, and you seem to freeze at these plateaus forever. There was one point in my own program where I appeared to be making no progress. At that time I was working on holding statistics in my mind, and calling them up at will. I stayed at one point for almost a month and a half, and since this was early in my training, I was very disappointed. By the end of the month I was working at it almost an hour and a half every night. It took every bit of my willpower to keep going, and then all of a sudden I had it. I almost doubled my ability to hold statistical data in my mind. It was a mind-boggling experience, and many of you will have similar experiences if, when you reach these plateaus, you stick to your practice. Plateaus are often the spring boards for tremendous leaps forward. Don't become discouraged. If you hang in there and continue to give it your best, you will progress. Many of the people who went through this training had become very discouraged because they'd been told when they were in school that they were second-raters. They weren't told exactly that—they were simply given IQ scores or other meaningless marks. It is particularly unfair because those marks depend to a large degree on the person's ability to concentrate, and since most young people had never been taught how to concentrate, they scored poorly. I have no doubt that when you increase your ability to concentrate, you increase your performance on all those so-called intelligence tests. So, no matter what level you performed at in school, don't be discouraged. We had dozens of young people who were doing mediocre and in some cases even failing work in college who went on to be A and B students after several months of training. They did so with ease and, of course, a great sense of joy and accomplishment. Don't quit.

If the very nature of your job precludes your using it as a measure of your ability to concentrate, you can measure your ability in other ways. One of the simplest is to take complex printed material dealing with your field and test yourself on it. Obviously, the complexity of the printed material will vary from page to page and from book to book, so the testing will not be simple, but you still can make a good estimate of how much you can read and absorb in a measured period of time. Of course, you can do better if you're a student and the material that you want to test is in textbooks, because they're written on a uniform level. Which means you can test your ability to concentrate by simply starting on page 1 of Chapter 1 and seeing how far you get before you're interrupted, and then continuing to measure in the same way throughout the book.

If you start building any set of muscles or practicing any skill, including the ability to concentrate, it's best if you exercise or practice on a regular basis. Any coach will tell you, whether you're practicing to run or to lift weights, that you'll do better if you have a schedule, because random practice is not as effective. I suggest you start with a period of fifteen minutes every day during which you measure and practice your ability to concentrate. If you are able to concentrate for fifteen minutes without interruption, or anywhere close to that, you may immediately expand your time to a half hour. When you reach that, you can go to three quarters of an hour, an hour, and so on. You won't get past an hour, though, until you become an accomplished mental weight lifter, and some people will never make it. But if you practice you will improve, and you will improve dramatically. As a result, you'll be able to perform almost any task more effectively.

Training Yourself to Focus

Only after you have developed a pattern of practice for concentration should you start working on focus. It isn't that working on focus is difficult; in fact, it's very simple. It's because practicing to concentrate is so difficult that we don't want anything to interfere with it.

When I first started teaching my employees to focus, I was delighted, because their productivity increased by leaps and bounds. The ability to focus is the linchpin of productivity. Everything else depends on it. I've run across a number of people who never developed the ability to concentrate for long periods of time, and who are nevertheless very effective workers, because they've learned to focus.

Over a period of several years we tried dozens of methods of practicing focus, but the one that worked best for the most people was blocking, the method used by the cults to control their members. If you get into an airport and ask one of those young people selling flowers any of the questions the cult doesn't want him to answer, the question will not register. If you ask him where his parents live, or if he's called home lately, or does he really think the guru owns cannon factories, he will block. Most of them go into a chant, some chant aloud and some chant to themselves, but all the chants serve the same purpose—blocking out the question and the questioner. The chant usually runs something to the effect that what's-his-name is God, everything what's-his-name says is true, what's-his-name protects me from the devil, and if you're asking the question, you're identified as the devil. The cults condition these young people to go into these chants through extensive training or brainwashing sessions. Every time a taboo subject is brought up during these training sessions, everyone chants. After a very short period of time, as soon as they hear any of those subjects, they go into their chant, and it works.

You can use exactly the same method to teach yourself to focus. Simply sit around and think of the times you've drifted off during work, and every time you think of one of those times, chant "back to work, back to work, back to work, back to work." Keep imagining yourself breaking focus, and thinking of all those things that make you break focus, and the minute you think of one of them, say, "back to work, back to work, back to work." Since most of us work in public, I suggest that you practice a nonverbal chant. After all, you don't want yourself shouting out "back to work" in the office. It might be embarrassing, and your boss might come out and ask you the very legitimate question why you stopped in the first place.

In addition to helping you maintain focus, the "back to work" chant, we found, cuts down on the number of times you break concentration. Apparently, if your subconscious knows that the chant is there ready to force you back to work, you're less likely to let small things disturb you. We found that once the chant became silent and instant, it seemed to prevent people from breaking concentration. It snapped them back to work so quickly that they hardly noticed the break, which means the break was so small it couldn't be measured. Going back to work as soon as your concentration starts to break can become a conditioned reflex, which will make it easy for you to maintain focus; and once you do this, you become a great worker.

Mechanical Aids

In addition to this very simple but effective method, we developed several mechanical devices that work quite well. In an attempt to study exactly what went on when my co-workers and I broke focus, I ran videotapes in my office. I found that when I allowed my concentration to be broken, I leaned back in my chair, and it was only after I leaned back that I broke focus. It was only in this relaxed position that I allowed my mind to fly out the window or onto subjects I didn't want to be thinking about. When I leaned forward and pulled my body erect, I invariably went back to work. Once I realized this, I came up with a little device to help myself keep focus. I took a battery, a red light, a buzzer, and two wires, and attached them to the metal spring of my chair. The minute I leaned back the two wires made contact, and the buzzer and the red light went on. After a week I removed the buzzer because it was too much of a distraction, but I left the little red Christmas bulb on my desk, and every time it blinked I said, "back to work, back to work," and that's what I did. I went back to work.

When I saw how well this simple device worked for me, I videotaped as many people as I could and found out that almost everyone had physical activities connected with breaking concentration. As a result we developed a whole series of mechanical signals. One fellow took off his glasses when he lost concentration, so we put a little red sign inside the bridge of his glasses, which he couldn't see while he was wearing them, but which popped right into sight when he took them off. It said, not surprisingly, "back to work." Another fellow put a rubber band on his glasses, and when he went to take them off, they bounced back against his head. I thought that was a bit drastic, but it worked. A woman who worked for me took off her shoes every time she broke concentration. She started wearing shoes that were strapped or laced, and it helped. In fact, in almost every case these simple devices helped.

Taken in isolation, each of these little exercises and devices seems simple. But the fact is this chapter is really a chapter on mental calisthenics. It will require enormous effort on your part if it is to affect your life positively. Don't become discouraged. Remember, doing mental calisthenics is much like doing physical calisthenics. Initially there will be aches and pains, and it will take tremendous stamina to stick with the exercises, but you'll reach a point where mental calisthenics become as enjoyable to you as physical calisthenics are to those who lift weights. In fact, you could become addicted to these exercises. Many do once they become good at them.

This is the chapter that is most likely to turn you, the reader, off. It's the chapter that asks the most of you, but it's also the chapter that can give you the most if you stick to it. Hang in there.

CHAPTER EIGHT

Creativity

Early Research

Every time the subject of creativity comes up, I think of eating cioppino at Scoma's, a very fine fish restaurant on the San Francisco docks. From that moment to this, the subject that fills this chapter has filled a good number of my waking hours. The study of creativity has gone from an assignment I really didn't want to a lifelong hobby and passion.

The lunch was to celebrate the end of a very successful job. A friend had hired me to help him package his company's latest computer. I had researched its name, and the color and design of the cabinet. After his third glass of wine, my friend confessed that I almost didn't get the job. He said that, although his partners were now delighted with my work, when he first suggested hiring me they almost strung him up. It seems several years before they had hired a psychologist consultant to help them recruit more creative engineers from college campuses. At the time they were recruiting from the best schools, paying top dollar, and in theory should have been getting the best engineers money could buy; but they weren't. Most of the engineers they recruited turned out to be bright, but unimaginative plodders; and they thought that, with all the time, effort, and money they were putting into their recruiting program, they should be getting a higher percentage of creative types. Two of the partners had worked for one of the giants in the field, and they said that when they started at their previous companies, they had been given a very complicated battery of psychological tests, which they believed were at least partially geared to identifying creativity. Since they were now competing head on with that giant, they decided to hire the psychologist to develop a similar battery of tests for them.

When they used his tests, the results were disastrous. Instead of attracting one or two creative engineers every year, as they had been doing for some time, their batting average dropped to zero. After two years they dropped the test and their belief in consultants. Somewhere toward the end of the lunch, one of the partners who had originally hired that consultant asked me if I would take a look at the consultant's work. He said that my work was so much better than the consultant's that he thought I could do something positive with the data the consultant had collected. He still believed there was a possibility of recruiting more creative people right out of college if they went about it the right way, and thought that if I looked at the research, I'd probably come to different conclusions than the first man. I told him that it wasn't my field and I didn't want to become involved, but he insisted. After several minutes of coaxing, I gave in, or at least I seemed to. I said I would look at the earlier work and give him my opinion, but do it without charging the company. It was my way of putting him off, and that's exactly what I meant to do: sit down, skim through the first man's work, and make an offhand comment. Instead, when I started reading, I became so fascinated that the subject captured me, and I've been involved in the study of creativity ever since.

The questionnaire that had been developed by the psychologist consultant wasn't any different from other questionnaires being used at the time. It was based on the best work available, and when I looked at the research, I drew exactly the same conclusions he had. The only difference was that he accepted the research at face value, and I questioned its validity from the very beginning. Although it met all the criteria for academic validity, which is the standard measure applied to research by most professionals, it was obvious to me that the research didn't do what it set out to do. As a man who had to invent his own research techniques to investigate the nonverbal signals of clothing, I understood that new areas of research require innovative techniques, and I didn't see any.

When I went back and looked at the studies the earlier consultant had used to develop his questionnaire, I decided they could be divided into four groups. First, there were essays by psychologists on the subject of creativity, which were interesting documents, but not very enlightening. A degree in psychology is used by many people as a license to guess. Their guesses are accepted by many as long as they're couched in psychological terms and surrounded with something that sounds vaguely like research. These guesses are usually the basis for theories on creativity that are widely held by and disseminated in the popular press.

Second, he used real world research. There were studies based on interviews and observations of creative people. These were by far the best works on creativity. At first glance they seemed not only interesting but very informative. However, on closer examination there were several obvious flaws. The first and most basic was that the people the researchers chose to interview, in my humble opinion, were not always creative. More often than not, when the studies were conducted by academics, they interviewed other academics, and when the studies were underwritten by corporations, the list of creative people was overloaded with corporate executives. But at least those studies had some validity, because the people doing the interviewing had some idea what the people who were being interviewed had accomplished.

The silliest studies fall into the third group—those based on interviews with the people I refer to as the instantly creative. Many of the studies identified creative people as those who chose to join creative "professions"— actors, painters, artists. It is ludicrous to assume that everyone who works in a creative field is creative, but that was the assumption. It is equally ridiculous to believe that successful actors, painters, and sculptors are creative, because success has little or nothing to do with creativity. I'm not saying that poets, essayists, and actors aren't creative; many of them are. The reason I chose not to interview large numbers of them is that it's very difficult to spot which ones are and which ones aren't creative. Often a poet or a painter who is considered a genius in his own lifetime is looked upon by the next generation as a hack. History is resplendent with examples of men and women who were ignored and even vilified by their own age, but recognized as universal geniuses after they died. Therefore, I only interviewed a handful of people in the arts, and only those whose accomplishments were so enormous that their fame seemed bound to continue after their demise.

The fourth group that these researchers mistakenly interviewed were public creative heroes. These are people who everyone knows are creative, and they are bent on defending their creative images. I consider some of their statements to be questionable at best, and sometimes just misleading. When they were being interviewed, they seemed more interested in their own PR than in contributing to the study.

Once I decided to interview creative people, I also decided it would be better to interview fewer people, who almost everyone agreed were creative, than a large number whose creativity could be questioned. I chose to interview eighty-seven people who were identified by leaders in their field as being creative and innovative. In each case I insisted that the person identifying them tell me exactly what they did and why it represented a breakthrough. I also insisted that this value judgment be supported by two or three other people in the field. The purpose of these interviews was a limited one. I wished to see if these creative people had any characteristics in common, so that the company who was paying for the research could identify similar people when they were still in college.

The reason this company was so interested in identifying creative engineers while they were still in college was that they come at bargain prices. A young creative engineer just out of college commands only a fraction of the salary you would have to pay to get the same engineer four years later if he has established a reputation as an innovator, and then you'll be lucky to get him. The reason this is important is that hiring creative people has become critical to corporate profits and survival. This is particularly true for a corporation in the high-tech industries. Creativity has become the most valuable product of corporate America in the last twenty years. If a company or a nation is to be productive today, it must be creative. Both companies and nations must foster and encourage creativity, particularly among their technical people, because creativity is all that stands between them and bankruptcy. In today's world, where capital can and does flow from country to country and continent to continent with the rapidity of electronic impulse, the real strength and wealth of nations and corporations depends on the productivity of their work force. And one of the essential elements of this productivity is creativity. In fact it is the only essential element of productivity in which we as a people still have a lead, but that lead is quickly evaporating.

How We Chose Our Subjects

My interviews with creative people were different from others in several ways. First, the creative people I chose were mainly from small corporations, and they were almost all technicians. Their creativity was a matter of fact, not a matter of opinion. Most of them had a specific item they had developed that they could, or their friends could and did, point to. Second, they were people who had agreed to be interviewed because they were interested in contributing to the subject, not because they were interested in blowing their own horn. The way I guaranteed this was to have all my subjects sign a nondisclosure agreement. I did this because I found that many public creative types, Nobel laureates, etc., were really interested in media attention, and made themselves very accessible to the media. They were easy to interview, because they were interested in increasing their value as public speakers, TV personalities, or intellectual heroes. Naturally, with this perspective, they maintained that their creativity was a gift of the gods. It was something that couldn't be explained, which meant that they were superior beings with a gift that no one else had, and that no one else could even discuss. This, of course, made every word that fell from their mouths golden. Their motives became transparent the minute I asked them to sign the nondisclosure agreement, because at that point many of them refused to be interviewed. I had had exactly the same experience when I interviewed top executives from American corporations for my earlier books. I found that there were a number of them who wouldn't give an interview unless they were sure they were going to get publicity. For them, an interview was nothing more than a public relations opportunity.

In addition, I only interviewed creative people who thought that creativity might be teachable. I didn't insist that they believed that it could be taught, but simply that they thought it was possible that through instruction, conditioning, or both we could take a percentage of the population, possibly including themselves, and make them more creative. Finally, I conducted nonstructured interviews, and I conducted them personally, because it takes a great deal of skill to conduct such interviews. A nonstructured interview is one in which only a few general points are introduced by the interviewer. The person being interviewed really controls the subject matter. I wanted creative people to discuss creativity in their own terms. I did this because, when I read some of the earlier studies, I found that they were often premise-oriented, and I didn't often agree with the premise.

Two Myths About Creativity

I had great problems with two recurring premises. The first was that creative people are open to all new ideas. I found that this simply isn't true. To be creative, people only have to be open to new ideas in their fields. I interviewed many creative men and women who were very conservative and lived very traditional lives. Their beliefs were products of their backgrounds, not their creativity. Those who were at the far left of the political spectrum came from homes and backgrounds where most others were from the far left, and those who were to the far right usually had parents who were from the far right. Like the rest of us, most were somewhere in the middle; they didn't have easily categorized political, philosophical, or religious beliefs. There was a somewhat bohemian attitude among many creative people; however, I often wondered which came first, the chicken or the egg. Did they become bohemian because they were creative and thought that's how they should be, or did they become creative because they were bohemian? There are enough people who live traditional life-styles to leave the question open. Many of them, even the so-called bohemians, never tried new foods—we found a lot of steak and potatoes people. And they were certainly not into fashion. Being chic or with it or up to date was something they cared little or nothing about.

The second premise that bothered me was that creativity was a gift of the gods. As strange as it may sound, there were researchers who set out with the premise that creativity was not researchable. You could tell if you read the interviews very carefully that they were delighted to have pleasant and entertaining conversations with interesting people. They weren't out to discover any underlying truth, and since they were out to prove nothing, that's exactly what they proved. A good researcher must assume that he can discover an undiscovered truth. It is an essential characteristic of all creative people that they are positive, and that they believe that all things are possible. That is also the first and primary prerequisite of a good researcher.

The Relationship Between Intelligence and Creativity

The first conclusion that I came to is that creative people are very intelligent. This may seem self-evident, but obviously it's not, because the premise on which much of the earlier research was based, particularly the work done by noncreative academic types, is that there is no correlation between intelligence and creativity. I was so surprised by this that I interviewed a few people who conducted this research, and I found that they were protecting their egos.

Their reasoning ran something like this: "I'm a college professor with my Ph.D. and my friends all have Ph.D.'s, and we were all brilliant students who had straight A's in school, and we haven't done anything creative. If bright people like us aren't creative, you must know that being bright and being creative aren't related." They go on to point out that there are people who are very creative, and who obviously aren't as intelligent as they. Of course, this is ridiculous. There is a far higher correlation between socioeconomic background and formal education than between intelligence and formal education, and there are all sorts of studies that indicate that IQ scores are a product of background as well. Which means that the creative blue-collar worker is probably far more intelligent than all of those uncreative college professors with their Ph.D.'s and high IQ scores.

It is simply a fact that creative people are intelligent and it's an obvious fact. If you go to the trouble of talking to creative people about the fields in which they made their breakthroughs, it's a fact that you can't escape. When they speak about their areas of expertise, their logic is impeccable and their feeling for development is superb, and they handle ideas with precision, which are all signs of intelligence. The real explanation of this apparent contradiction is that all of the uncreative sociology and psychology professors haven't come up with a good technique for measuring intelligence, and therefore they miss the entire point. The ability to see things differently first requires that you see them as everyone else sees them. Creativity demands understanding the essence of a problem, and therefore intelligence is the essential element in that process. The first thing that I told the company I worked for was, if they wanted to hire creative people, they should check their IQ scores, because as imperfect as the scores are, they are the only measurement we have of intelligence and there is a definite correlation between intelligence and creativity.

And since they were hiring engineers, all of whom have gone through at least sixteen years of formal education, in comparison the IQ scores would have a greater validity than would those of a cross section of the public.

I must put in a word of warning. If you're going to use IQ tests to help identify creative people, you must make a socioeconomic adjustment. You must do this because IQ scores have an economic bias. If you're testing people for creativity and using IQ scores alone, you're going to miss your mark. You must take the IQ scores and then factor in the subjects' backgrounds. Off the top of my head, I would subtract 10 points from the IQ scores of any college professor on the premise that his educational background adds 10 points, and I would add 10 points or even 15 points to the IQ score of a poor black from the ghetto, because his socioeconomic environment penalizes him at least 15 points. Which means that if there was a 20- to 30-point spread in IQ between a professor and a ghetto kid, they'd probably be equal in ability.

How Much Perspiration, How Much Inspiration

The second characteristic of creative people is they're hard and effective workers. They know how to work, and they like to work. They have all the characteristics of good workers. They're usually marathon workers. They often spend long hours doing what they do. In fact, many work all the time. They never turn off. They take their work with them wherever they go. They stick with a project until it's completed, sometimes for years. I think that creativity sometimes takes more guts and stick-to-itiveness than brains. In addition to working hard, creative people have a unique sense of organization. They may not seem to be organized, because they're always juxtaposing seemingly unrelated ideas, but they are organized because it takes a very strong innate sense of order to do that. They create by bringing order to seeming disorder, or seeing a new order where there was none. They're always thinking, rethinking, reviewing, and reordering.

By the way, the fact that creativity and work are related is almost never brought up by noncreative types. They believe that creativity is a product of inspiration and that that is a gift of the gods. Creative people nearly always relate creativity to hard work. In fact, we asked a number of them who they would prefer to work with on a creative project: two people with 150 IQ's, both at the top of their class, both wonderful engineers or scientists who would work eight hours a day, or two people with 120 IQ's, just a little above average for college graduates, who are willing to work sixteen to twenty hours a day. Almost all of them said that they would prefer the people with the 120 IQ's. Edison's comment that creativity is 99 percent perspiration and 1 percent inspiration is a feeling shared by most creative people. Only uncreative people, and that includes the majority of those who conduct most of the research, ignore or underestimate the relationship between perspiration and creativity. When you talk to creative people about how they create, all they talk about is hard work. They are annoyed by the idea that creativity is a type of miracle. Inspiration from the gods is something they recognize, but they have problems with it. If they had a motto, it would be "Try, try, and try again, and if you still haven't succeeded, you're not trying hard enough."

The reason that noncreative researchers tend to overlook the work element in creativity is, again, they're protecting themselves, and their very easily bruised egos. They believe they work hard, and yet they're not creative, and therefore, work isn't essential to creativity, or at least it isn't a key element. The fact is creative people work harder than noncreative people. There's another reason uncreative researchers are led astray. Creative people often seem not to be working, but, instead, looking off into space, staring out a window, or watching television. When noncreative types look into space, stare out a window, or watch television, they see stars, people walk past, or the six o'clock news. When creative types look into space, stare out the window, or watch television, they see the future.

Positive Creative Attitude

The third characteristic of creative people is they're positive. This characteristic was displayed by almost everyone we interviewed. The story that demonstrates it best concerns two professors. They work at different universities, in two different fields; both have made breakthroughs, and both told almost identical stories. Each said that there was a member of his department who was extremely bright and extremely jealous of him, because that person hadn't made a breakthrough. Each said that this very bright person was the most negative person he knew, and each used the noncreative bright co-worker to check his research—both of them in exactly the same way. When either had what he thought was a creative idea, he immediately went to his uncreative co-worker and bounced it off him. The minute that uncreative person heard the new idea, he thought of every reason it wouldn't work. Each professor said that person was so good at being negative that he eliminated all the nonsense. (If there was a flaw in their premise, these brilliant negative people would point it out and save the professors from wasting their time.) They also said that a negative attitude can never work. It was the thing that stopped the bright people from being creative. One paraphrased Henry Ford when he said, "If you believe you can solve a problem or if you believe you can't, you're probably right."

We found that creative people had as many worries about the future of the world as noncreative people. In fact more, because they were more intelligent, but they believe in a future. If you ask them if man will ever solve the problem of feeding all the billions of people likely to be on Earth, most of them will say he probably will. They're not sure how—new seeds, outer-space farming, or who knows what—but they think it's possible, because they think everything is possible. They're optimists. If you ask creative and uncreative types if we'll colonize the moon, they'll both say yes, because this is a commonly held belief. But if you ask creative and uncreative people if we'll colonize the other solar systems, most creative people will say yes, while most noncreative people will say probably not. When the noncreative people say probably not, they often sound more intelligent than the creative people, because they give you wonderful reasons why we can't—distance, time, space— but the simple fact is that they don't have the faith, the optimism, and the positive outlooks of creative people. Creative people don't necessarily believe in a bright future, but they do believe in an unlimited future. The main difference between creative and uncreative people when they think about the future is that creative people try to deal with it. They may be able to outline exactly what they think is going to happen when the world is blown up by atomic bombs, and they can go into enormous detail about how horrible it's going to be, but the fact is they're always thinking about the possible. Almost invariably, if you ask them if this must happen, they'll say no, it's always possible something else can take place. This is one of the reasons that we advised our corporate clients when interviewing college students to ask them about the future of their fields—to ask them what they think is going to happen in twenty or thirty years. Creative students usually have an answer. Their answers may seem silly to the experts, who are often on the cutting edge of the research, but that's not important. What is significant is that they worked out a theory. The theory may make them look foolish, but that really is a good sign, because uncreative people will do anything to avoid looking foolish. If you ask uncreative people the same question, they'll give you a "depends" answer—it depends on this, or it depends on that—which means they're really avoiding answering the question. If you ask them about this, they'll tell you the real reason they can't give you an answer is that they never thought about the question. Creative people, on the other hand, are future people. They're always interested not only in tomorrow, but in the day after, and they enjoy playing with ideas of what will be, what can be, and what is possible.

Creative people are also in love with the idea of creating, and for many it is the most important thing in life. They want to be around others who create and they want to have an opportunity to create themselves. If they have two job offers, one that promises high pay, security, and enormous benefits with no chance to create, and the other whose offer is moderate pay and benefits with a chance to experiment and play with ideas, in most cases they'll choose the second. Now, they're not fools: if someone offers them $40,000 a year while someone else offers $20,000, they'll in most cases opt for the $40,000 because they can see many creative things to do with the other $20,000. But when the pay offers and benefit offers are at all close, the company that offers them a chance to do something creative has a tremendous advantage. This is why small companies have an advantage over large ones when recruiting creative people: small outfits can offer creative people the freedom to experiment. Another reason small companies have an advantage in attracting creative people is that although creative people are dreamers, they're also doers.

They want to do and they want to do it now. They're always in a hurry, they want to control something at this moment, not five years from now or ten years from now. Uncreative people can wait, because they believe that they're never going to do anything anyway.

Creative Adults Were Lonely Children

Finally we told our corporate clients to speak to their future engineers about their childhood. In the past, corporations tried to hire outgoing people—cheerleaders, captains of the football team, etc. That's terrific if you're hiring a salesperson, but it's not terrific if you're trying to hire a creative engineer. Of the eighty-seven people we talked to, eighty-five of them said they had not been particularly happy children. Over 70 percent of those identified as creative said that at some time during their childhood they felt isolated. The reasons for their isolation were many and varied. Some admitted to being socially inept, others lived in environments where no one understood them; some were very bright people and intellectually deprived in their environment, several were sick as children, and a few lived in areas where there was nothing to do. Of the eighty-seven, only two were the American ideal, healthy, outdoor, athletic types brought up in suburbia, captain of the football team and so on. Both were men and both told similar stories. Their families at one time couldn't afford a second car. Their fathers took the only car to work, and when the boys got home from school, as much as it killed them, they couldn't go out with the rest of the kids, because they didn't have transportation. As a result, both said they spent hours in their rooms thinking and playing with ideas, and both thought that this was a critical changing point in their creative lives. Among the eighty-seven people questioned, only six identified themselves as being popular, and four of these were women. Since we only interviewed twelve women, popularity and creativity among women may not be related.

These young people not only had a sense of isolation from their peers, often they were isolated within the family unit as well. They were likely to be only children or to have been separated by at least several years from their brothers and sisters. Most of them admitted that they had only a few friends. I think, even after all these years, they were giving themselves the benefit of the doubt. As I saw it, they were people who for one reason or another, between the ages of seven and fourteen, learned to entertain themselves with their own thoughts, or to live in the world of ideas.

When I finished the research I passed the results on to my friend's company even though he was no longer there, and I felt a bit guilty thinking that this research was probably not any more useful than the research done by the first consultant. It wasn't until seven years later, when I started writing this book, that I knew I had struck gold. When I went to the company and asked them if I could publish the information three months before I had the right to do so, they said absolutely not; and, although I didn't challenge their right to say no, they went to the trouble of having a lawyer contact me and threaten me. When I asked him why they were so upset, he told me that the company believed the information was valuable enough that they should deny publishing rights for three months so that they could continue to have the use of the information exclusively for even that short period of time. Apparently they had had tremendous luck hiring creative engineers using my questions.

Although that project had been very informative and enlightening and apparently useful, I was not happy with it. What it really did was get me involved in the field of creativity. Although the research itself didn't constitute a breakthrough, during the last interview I made a wonderful discovery.

Family and Friends

I was on a book tour and had arranged with my publisher to have the tour end in Miami. I wanted to stay at the Diplomat Hotel with my wife for a couple of days and lie in the sun. Instead, on the final day of the tour, the weather turned cold and I drove to Orlando. On the way I interviewed a college professor who had made a breakthrough in his field and had agreed to be one of my subjects. The only reason I interviewed him was that I happened to be driving past, and that's the reason he was the last person on the list as well. When I met him in his laboratory, he introduced me to his assistant, who is also his wife, and since my wife was with me, I invited both of them to join us for lunch. As soon as we finished the meal I started the interview, and while I was conducting what I considered a very serious interview, my wife and his were sitting at the end of the table laughing and pointing at us. I ignored them and asked the last half-dozen questions about lifestyle. He told me he was a very normal husband and father, and that he lived a very normal life. As soon as I finished my questioning I tuned into the women's conversation, and to my surprise, though he had been telling me how normal he was, his wife was describing him as a nut, and my wife was giving the same description of me. My wife complained that she had put up her own money for a trip to Acapulco, taken me to the beach, made sure I had no pad, no pen, and no work, and found me doing statistics in the sand. His wife, in an "I can top that one," said that she had a bigger problem. A few nights earlier she had taken her husband to a dinner party, and found him writing something on the tablecloth. She said she had never been so embarrassed and humiliated in her life, and she wanted to crown him. At that point in the conversation both of our wives looked at us with disbelief, and all of a sudden I realized that most of the information I had gathered about creative people was probably inaccurate. It was inaccurate because I had just asked a creative professor about his life-style, and if you had asked me, I would have given the same answers. Both the professor and I maintained that we were ordinary people, and yet our wives described us as screwballs. I decided right then and there that I would interview a new group of creative people and that in addition to interviewing them, I'd interview their spouses. Once I started doing these multiple interviews, I extended the list to include boyfriends and girlfriends, both homosexual and heterosexual, parents, peers, childhood friends, neighbors, siblings, and anyone else I could lay my hands on. I very quickly came to the conclusion that in the opinion of most people around them, creative people are very strange, and that the opinions of people around them are probably accurate.

Logical Nonconformity

It became evident after just a few interviews that creative people are nonconformists—but a special type of nonconformists, pragmatic nonconformists. They do not conform to the rules and regulations laid down by society when those rules and regulations do not make much sense. They're always looking for reasons, and if they don't see a good reason for doing something a certain way, the fact that everyone else does it that way isn't a sufficient reason. They're always looking for logic. For example, one of the signs of creativity seems to be nonconformity in dress, and I recognized this after interviewing only a few people. When I asked them why they dressed the way they did, most gave me the same answer. They explained that the function of clothing was to protect them from the elements and prevent them from getting arrested, and that as long as clothing performed those two functions, in their opinion it could be as comfortable and inexpensive as possible, and that they dressed the way they did because the clothing they wore did exactly what they wanted it to do. In some cases they looked like kooks, and when I explained to them that their clothing, in addition to protecting them from the elements, also sent a message about them to other people, and that by controlling their clothing they could control the message and to a degree control the way other people treated them, although some scoffed most were interested. They were particularly impressed when I pointed out that I was a researcher and used my image to help me raise money and to get contracts, which gave me a chance to do more research. The minute they saw a practical function for clothing, many were willing to change. In fact, several asked me for copies of my *Dress for Success* book so they could get started right away.

We again saw this characteristic of logical nonconformity when they dealt with problems, not just the problems in their fields, but everyday problems which they solved differently than the rest of the world. I ran across dozens of stories that demonstrated this. One concerned a well-known writer who purchased a new home. When he moved in, he and his wife discovered that four of the windows in the house leaked. His wife arranged to have someone come and caulk the windows the next day, but since she had to go out and it looked like it was going to rain, she told him he was going to have to watch the windows. If it started to rain, he'd have to put towels under each window to soak up the water, so that the floors and the ceiling beneath wouldn't be damaged. Which meant if it rained, he was going to have to run from one window to another with towels and mops. When the writer's wife came home, she found cookie sheets hanging out all four windows. The writer, being a creative person, went right to the heart of the problem. As he saw it, the problem was water dripping inside the house, and since that could be solved if he could redirect the water, he simply looked for a way of doing that. The first thing he ran across was cookie sheets, and he decided if he put them in the windows at a proper angle, the water would run down the cookie sheets and drop outside the house. Of course, it made the house look very strange to anyone who didn't know what was going on, and the neighbors probably thought the man was crazy; but the solution was wonderful—it worked.

Creative people often solve ordinary problems in very unusual ways. When the writer's wife started to tell him that nobody in his right mind would do that, she immediately stopped. She knew that that argument had no validity for him, and it doesn't have validity for most creative people. The fact that no one else does it doesn't mean anything. Creative people have tremendous egos. They believe in themselves, not the world. The fact that this man's neighbors might think he was crazy didn't bother him, and it wouldn't bother most other creative people. All their lives they've understood that the world doesn't understand them, and they've come not to expect understanding. Because they don't expect understanding, they really don't expect applause and they don't worry about being booed.

Another wife told a similar story. There was an unsightly dead bush in the garden, and she kept nagging her husband to dig it up and throw it out. She asked him time and again, and finally one day he threw up both hands in exasperation and said okay, he'd do it. While she watched, he took a shovel, dug into the earth once or twice, and then walked away. She said she was so mad she didn't even go after him; she just went back into the kitchen assuming he had quit. Twenty minutes later she heard a crashing sound in the yard. When she ran out she saw that her husband had borrowed the neighbor's four-wheel drive, taken the tow chain, wrapped it around the bush, and pulled the bush out of the ground. To him this was a perfect solution. It was quicker and easier than digging. When she ran up to the car and told him no normal person would do it that way, he looked at her and said, "Normal people are stupid." This is simply another case where the "It's not normal" or "Everybody wouldn't do it that way" argument didn't wash. Creative people aren't worried about the other fellow. They only worry about their own sense of logic.

During the original eighty-seven interviews, I talked to creative people mainly about the contributions they'd made in their own fields. In order to do so, I had to research music, computers, literature, and a series of other areas in an attempt to understand the significance of the contribution made by each person. Frankly, in most cases my research was inadequate to the task. In order to appreciate what people at the cutting edge of their fields are really doing, you have to understand their fields, and in most cases I didn't have the time to develop that type of expertise, and neither do most of the people who do the research on creativity. That's their flaw, that's the reason why learning that creative people have a creative mind-set that applies to every task was an important breakthrough. It let me look at how their minds work without having to understand their often very complicated contributions.

I don't want to lead you astray and let you believe that what the husbands, lovers, and wives of creative people said was really the key to creativity. It wasn't—the key was what creative people said themselves. However, the remarks of spouses, family, and friends formed a background tapestry that let me understand what creative people were really saying, instead of what they appeared to be saying. As a result of over 1500 hours of interviews with creative people, and over 800 hours of interviews with their wives, husbands, lovers, and so on, I believe I have a handle on the subject. I've come to the conclusion that creativity has four elements—problem, expertise, emotional involvement, and solution—and that understanding these steps can help us all become more creative.

The Four Elements of Creativity

A classic story of creativity, which displays all four elements, is the Archimedes story. Hero, king of Syracuse, purchased a new gold crown. He suspected that the gold had been adulterated, so he called in Archimedes and told him he wanted to find out if it was a pure gold crown without destroying it. This obviously was the first stage of creativity—the setting up of a problem.

Archimedes was called in by the king because he was a scientist and mathematician, and volume and mathematics were an intimate part of his world. He knew gold was the heaviest metal, and that if he could find the volume of the crown, he could compare it to pure gold, and tell whether it was pure. He didn't have to think about that. That information was at his fingertips. What he needed was a breakthrough. He had to discover how to measure the volume of that very irregularly shaped crown. Archimedes's situation illustrates why most people who make creative breakthroughs do not believe in accidental creativity. They admit that occasionally a person looking for solution X may solve problem Y, but they insist that in almost every case the person had intimate knowledge of problem Y even though he was looking for the solution to problem X. Therefore, they believe that you must be an expert in a field in order to make a creative breakthrough. You have to be intimately involved in a field in order to have the resources for the quantum leap that's called creativity. This is the reason poetry is not written by physicists. Even if a physicist has a wonderful command of the English language and understands all the rules of metrics, he's not likely to write great poetry because poetry is not the driving force of his life. This does not mean that poetry can't or won't be written by anyone who isn't a professional poet. If poetry is your hobby and you have an intimacy with the information, then it's possible you may write poetry, but only if that intimacy dominates your mental activity. The intimacy that is expertise is the second characteristic of creativity.

The third characteristic of creativity is a love of problem solving. The creative people we interviewed enjoyed telling us how they went about solving problems. They even enjoyed telling about the mistakes they made and the false leads they followed and the dumb things they did. They enjoyed it in the same way a good detective enjoys telling about the dark alleys he went down and the false leads he followed before he solved a case. Creative people are intellectual detectives. They enjoy the search much more than they enjoy the solution, and the search for truth dominates their lives. The strangest things make the problems pop into their minds. As a result, the problems are always on their minds, or just below the surface. Solving their problems is a source of entertainment to them, and part of their lives. They never leave their problems at the office, they never turn off their brains, and that leads us back to Archimedes and the fourth element of creativity —solution.

When Archimedes stepped into the bathtub and saw the water overflow, he realized he had displaced his own volume and he's supposed to have yelled, "Eureka!" Meaning, "I have it!" He had the solution. The reason he had come up with the solution at that moment is that the problem was right in front of him. He was ready for that breakthrough. The emotional attachment he had for the problem held it ever in the front of his mind. The only similar experience I can think of is that of people who are in love with someone who is not present, or people who've had someone they love die. People in these emotional states will often be reminded of that missing party by all sorts of things. Songs, smells, tastes, words, scenery, a piece of furniture, will bring that person popping into their mind. It's the strong emotional involvement with that person at the moment that keeps bringing that person back onto the conscious level. It is a similar love affair—with missing solutions to a problem—that allows creative people to create, and it gives them a tremendous advantage.

Archimedes, if he had been a noncreative person, would have gone to the king, had the problem put before him, thought about it for an hour, two hours, three hours, or even a week, and if he hadn't come up with a solution by that time, that would have been the end of it. But being a creative person, Archimedes took the problem with him. He had an emotional involvement with it, which let him bring to bear on the problem everything in his environment, everything he felt, and everything he heard. When Archimedes saw the water flow over, he had an instant solution. However, his was not a typical creative solution. Most creative people do not have breakthroughs take place during the activities of the day. Some do and these are conscious solutions, but most creative people have what they call intuitive flashes or inspiration.

The Inspiration Trap

Intuition and inspiration are words that have lead more researchers on creativity down the garden path than have any others. They're words that only confuse, because when we think of intuition or inspiration, we think of an unexplained and unexplainable answer. Most researchers believe that creativity results from a flash of intuition—Archimedes jumping up and screaming "Eureka!" or the writer who all of a sudden gets the idea for the perfect novel—but that's not really what happens. If Archimedes had stepped into the bathtub with a beautiful woman, it is very unlikely that he would have thought of the king's crown, but at that time he would have had enough information in his subconscious to solve the problem. Since Archimedes was a creative person, the way the solution probably would have come to him is that late that night, lying in bed, or a week later sitting in front of the fireplace, while his mind was wandering and not thinking of much, all of a sudden the solution would have popped in full-grown. He might not have remembered the bathtub, or even the woman, and, if he remembered both, he might not have remembered why the bathtub and the woman were important to the solution; but he'd still have the solution. All that might have occurred to him is that when you put a crown in water, it's going to displace its own volume. What really would have happened is his mind would have solved the problem below the conscious level. When he saw the water overflow, his mind would have made the association without kicking it out.

An explanation for this that many creative people we interviewed liked was the computer analogy. Think of the mind as a computer with input, storage, processing, and a screen. Instead of the keyboard for putting in information, the mind computer takes in information it hears, smells, sees, tastes, and feels. The information is taken into the computer and is stored along with all other information that has ever been brought in the same way. The problem is part of the information. The internal workings of the computer have the ability not only to store information, but to rearrange it according to prearranged codes. If the person puts the problem in, and the information to solve it is present, the computer automatically processes it and says, "Solved—you have a solution." The screen is the conscious mind, which prints it out.

The screen's conscious mind prints what we're thinking of at the moment, whether it's a solution or not. If the computer brain takes in information that will solve the problem, but does so while the conscious mind or screen is on another problem, it can't print. The information simply won't come up on the screen, because there's only room for one thing on the screen at a time. But the mind will store the information. Unlike the standard computer, the mind screen and the internal workings of the mind never turn off. They're involuntary. So when the screen, or the conscious mind, is not being used, usually during a period of rest, it has the ability to kick out information, and that is why most creative people make breakthroughs late at night when they're sitting around seemingly unoccupied. It is in that state that the screen is empty and the solution pops onto the screen, that is, into conscious minds, fully solved.

Of course, this is not exactly what happens, but most of the creative people we spoke with agreed that it comes very close. It's the one explanation most of them felt most at home with. About 80 percent of them said that most researchers did not understand inspiration, that God doesn't touch them. They believe, as I do, that it's a type of subconscious problem-solving—problem-solving just below the conscious level.

If you accept these four elements of creativity, as most creative people do, then you can see that obviously you can work to develop certain areas. If you don't understand a problem or if you don't have a problem, or if you're not involved in solving problems, then you're never going to be creative. You have to identify a problem that you'd like to solve, and you have to make the positive statement that it's solvable and you're going to dedicate your time to it. Then, if you have the expertise that allows you to handle the problem, you are in the second stage. If you have to run to a book to look up iambic pentameter, you're not going to write sonnets. The beat must be part of your nature. In order to solve problems, you have to have a familiarity with information. Information, as I see it, exists on several levels. First is recall information: it takes a moment to recall things. Second is instant information: we know the information instantly. Third is reflex information: the information is so much a part of us that it's part of our nervous system. We instantly have this information. This is the type of information someone has when he dedicates his life to a field of study. It is usually this information that enables him to be creative. Therefore, the only advice we can give to people who are not experts is to become experts.

The third requirement for creativity is to become emotionally involved with a problem. Emotional involvement with a problem is something that you can foster in a series of ways. If you work at something you like, you're more likely to have an emotional attachment to it, and conversely if you work at a job you hate, you're less likely to have an emotional attachment or to be creative. But since the whole purpose of emotional attachment to an idea is to keep the idea near the surface of the mind so that the entire world in which you move can impact the problem, there are other ways of going about it.

Bringing Up the Problem

The first and simplest way is using an outside device to bring the problem close to the conscious mind. If you have a stopwatch that goes off every five minutes, you can use this to force a problem into your consciousness. People who have tried this say that the problem will never sink far below the conscious. This allows you to use your environment to help solve problems. It will give you the same advantage as the person who is emotionally attached to a problem. Several engineers who use this technique said that after several weeks they found they were far more creative. We had a second group of engineers, however, who complained that the alarm watch going off every five minutes disturbed them and made them less effective and less creative. For them we came up with a little device that blinked the problem on a screen in front of them so quickly that it was only picked up by their subconscious, a type of subliminal advertising. This device worked so well that they dubbed it the creativity box. They found that, without ever realizing why, the problem just popped into their minds over and over again, and that constantly having it in front of them made it much more easy for them to deal with it. It certainly kept it right below the conscious level, where it could be impacted by their environment, and two of the six we talked to said that they had made breakthroughs over the past several months due to the subliminal message-sending device.

Another technique we tried was hypnosis. We only had two engineers try this, but both claimed to have positive results. I was not involved with that unit of research, but I can report that it seemed to work. The fourth technique is the bulletin board method. One man had a problem which he wrote out on a rather large piece of paper; he had the paper reproduced fifty times and hung one copy on his desk, another in his bathroom at home, another in his kitchen, one next to his bed, and so on. Another technique that worked well was visualizing. Several people involved in problem-solving said that they visualized their problems at regular intervals. Whether visualization was set off by a stopwatch or another mechanical device did not seem to make a difference. These people would stop whatever they were doing for a minute and attempt to see their problems in front of them. One mathematician said that he kept closing his eyes and forcing himself to see the entire problem, not to try to solve it.

One of the things that divided the people who work in creative fields about these procedures is that some insisted that if they used them at work, it interfered with their productivity. Others used them all the time. Some used them exclusively during down hours. One man had his wristwatch go off every five minutes on his way home on the Long Island Railroad. Another man used the bulletin board device on his boat. He had copies of a problem he was dealing with hung all over the boat. A third engineer brought samples of the machinery he was working on at home and laid them not only on his desk in front of him, but on his kitchen table when he ate. He said that an intimacy with the hardware made solving the problem easier. The one thing that almost all of these people agreed on is that popping the information into their minds by any means gave them an intimacy with the problem that helped them discover solutions more easily. I don't know exactly how creative they were, but many claimed enormous creative successes.

Problem-Solving

The most interesting part of the creativity process is of course problem-solving, and it's particularly enticing to think that late one evening, when you're lying there doing nothing, a creative idea will simply pop into your mind. And the fact is—if you've prepared yourself properly—it might. In fact, it might even pop into your mind while you're asleep, although only two out of over four hundred creative people we interviewed on the subject said that they had had a breakthrough while asleep. Interestingly enough, at least half of them kept pencils and pads next to their beds just in case. They recognized that sleep and the state just before sleep is the time when they were most likely to have creative breakthroughs. I call this process *creative popping*. It happens at a time when the mind is at rest and lets ideas pop into the conscious that have already been stored in the subconscious. It's a skill that is very difficult to develop: you have to try not to try. You have to be completely relaxed and your mind has to be blank. Although we had only two subjects who tried hypnosis as part of the program, I interviewed several who said that hypnosis can help one arrive at this state, but as many said it could not. A number of people said they found that if before going to bed they did some light reading and then lay down and closed their eyes for a few minutes, it helped. One man found that drinking red wine often caused him to wake at night and that these were the times when he had his creative flashes. Another said that only when he stayed up until two or three in the morning and became totally exhausted did he ever make a breakthrough. Many of the people we questioned said that a state of relaxation that comes with exhaustion from work was the state in which they were creative. Understand that what I'm suggesting here may be impossible for a lot of people; however, I feel I must report it.

Finally, most of the creative people we talked to, even those who worked in isolation, said that there were positive and negative creative environments. The first aspect of a creative environment is a sounding board. They said that three creative people aren't three times as creative as one creative person. Sometimes they're ten times as creative.

Having colleagues with whom you can exchange ideas is often critical to creativity. This is why many of the most creative people in the country believe that working at a major university and being around others who are creative and brilliant is an advantage. However, the idyllic surrounding of the university, where everyone is cooperative and no one is competitive, is hardly the environment that most described. In fact, when most described their first creative breakthrough, they said it was a product of competition, if not jealousy. Time and again we've heard the story of a young talented person moving from a small unknown university or a small laboratory to a great university or a great laboratory, or moving from being a student to being a faculty member, and being for the first time exposed to the greats in his or her field. Intimacy of this type doesn't breed contempt, but competition. The former students start seeing the great men and women as ordinary people, and then they begin to believe that they are as smart as these great men and women, and as capable of making breakthroughs. Once they reach this point, they make a conscious determination to make breakthroughs and become one of them. Many said that their first creative contribution was ego-fueled. Ironically, a number of great scientists said that they believe that they lost their creativity with success, that when everyone started adoring them and treating them like creative geniuses, they no longer had the drive to create. In fact, one said that since creativity demanded risk-taking, and since once you become a public creative figure, it's much more difficult to take risks with your reputation, at that stage you're much less likely to be creative.

Risk-Taking

Which brings us to the next element of creativity—risk-taking—and the big risk is looking like a fool. If you're going to be creative, you're going to have to put your neck on the line. You have to take chances—it is essential. You may have to put your professional reputation and sometimes your career in jeopardy for an idea that isn't fully developed. You have to risk being laughed at. People everywhere laugh at geniuses, and you have to face the fact that, even if you make a breakthrough, it may cost you your credentials, your credibility, and your career. It has others. Several very creative people made the comment that risk-taking was part of youth, and so is creativity, and the older you become, the less likely you are to be creative. All the men who made this statement were in their fifties or older. Risk-taking is such an essential part of creativity that I almost called this chapter "Dare to Be Creative."

Idea-Popping

The area of creativity that we can help most is the area in which we would seem to be able to help least—inspiration. Our researchers discovered, as we said, that most inspirational flashes come to people who are relaxed and not at the moment involved in strenuous mental activity. Several dozen creative people we interviewed said that before their great ideas came, they'd had an inkling that they were about to make a breakthrough. One man said he knew he was on the verge of something big. Another said he knew something was going to happen, but he wasn't even sure what it was. He wasn't even sure it was connected with his work, but he knew something monumental would happen in his life. In fact, over 30 percent of the people who made breakthroughs said that, for a day or two or sometimes a week before, they knew they were on the edge of something. Possibly they already had the solution in their subconscious and it was fighting to get out. If you ever get that feeling, I believe you can increase your chance of making a breakthrough if you can create an environment that makes idea-popping probable. Since inspiration flashes come when your mind is unoccupied, you should set up a routine of light reading and resting or even taking a warm bath before you go to bed. In addition, you should have a pen and some paper or a recorder by your bed at all times, because almost everyone we spoke to said that they had creative ideas in the middle of the night that they lost, and they're not sure if they ever regained them. Then all you can do is wait and hope and take long leisurely walks or do anything else that helps you relax and takes no thought. Don't try for too long. A few days or a week is enough. After that it becomes counterproductive.

If you lose an idea, don't worry about it. Most people are not noncreative because they lose ideas; they're noncreative because they fail to act on the ideas they get. Of the people we interviewed who've made creative breakthroughs and who are leaders in their field, 80 percent indicated that after they had the breakthrough ideas, they had to work, sweat, and strive to take the abstract ideas and turn them into reality. The idea may be fully developed, but its presentation or its effectiveness usually is not. Creativity is undoubtedly more perspiration than inspiration. Almost everyone we spoke to said that the world is full of great ideas, but most people who have them don't act on them, and creativity requires action.

CHAPTER NINE

A Workers' Boot Camp

The All-American Boy

Twenty-five years ago I nicknamed him Jack Armstrong, the "All-American Boy!" So I'll call him Jack when I talk about him here. Using his real name probably would embarrass him and his company. I wouldn't do that for the world.

I called him Jack Armstrong for the obvious reasons. He was so clean-cut he squeaked, so upright he was almost unreal. When I first met him, Jack was twenty-eight, already had an M.B.A. from a leading university and was assistant to the president of a multimillion-dollar corporation. He contacted me because at the time I was writing articles for corporate magazines, and he was looking for a ghostwriter for his boss. Jack had everything going for him. He was good-looking, came from the right background, and it showed. He'd married a woman who came from an executive upper-middle-class background, had three very nice children, lived in a beautiful house in a good section of Long Island, and had already been chosen by the top people in his company as a young man on his way up. I'm not sure, but I'm willing to bet he was voted Most Likely to Succeed by his high-school class as well.

In spite of all his obvious virtues, I liked Jack. So did everyone else, and so would you if you met him. He is a very likable fellow, open, engaging, and good natured. He even imposed on people in ways that made you like him. Twenty-five years ago he called me one evening and told me that his babysitter had stood him up at the last moment, and that he was unable to find anyone else and he and his wife had to attend an important business function. He asked me to babysit. That may sound like a very ordinary request, except that he'd only met me half a dozen times before, and always in a business setting. Probably no one else I had known for that short a time could have talked me into traveling out to Long Island and sitting with three kids. At that time I was twenty-three, and when I was twenty-three I partied seven nights a week, and I didn't consider sitting with someone's children a party. But Jack was the type of fellow you found very hard to say no to, so I jumped into my car, drove out to his house, and stayed until two in the morning.

When I bumped into him twenty or so years later, he was, not unexpectedly, president of his company. When we got to talking, he told me he didn't move up directly in that company; he stayed four or five years after I first met him, and then he moved to another company, and finally, ten years before, he came back to the original company as executive vice president, and now he was the top man. As you've probably guessed, he was a very effective president. When he took over the company, its stock wasn't doing well, and now it was soaring. When we started talking, it was obvious that life, as usual, had been beautiful to Jack. If there were any bumps, they didn't show. His three children had graduated from top schools, one son was an attorney, another worked for a major corporation, and his daughter had a doctorate in economics and was teaching at a university. What annoyed me, however, was that he didn't look twenty years older. He looked about ten years older, which meant there had been a shift in our positions. When I saw him last, I looked five years younger than he. Now, he seemed to be five years younger than I. As I said, life smiled on Jack. Everything seemed to fall in place for him.

When we met in the hallway, for a second I didn't recognize him, but he recognized me immediately. He didn't know I was working for his company, or even what I did. Charming and considerate as ever, he invited me to lunch, and when he found out what I did, he showed great interest in the subject. I wasn't surprised. Jack always encouraged people to talk about themselves, and always listened intently, which makes everyone feel good. But this time he wasn't just being his usual polite charming self; he had good reason for listening. At that moment, he was involved in developing a long-term program to teach the executives in his company how to handle the media. In fact, he had just finished a training session. He was the first to take the recommended media course. He recognized that his company's image was a critical factor and affected its profits, and he had personally hired a young woman who had a great deal of television experience to teach him and the other executives how to handle themselves when they were on camera. Although he admitted he wasn't an expert, he thought he was developing into a polished TV personality. In fact, he had taped a program he was on, and when he played it for me, I had to admit he came off beautifully.

Beat Up on TV

About four months later I received a call from Jack and once again he asked me if I'd come out to his office. I told him I was no longer working for his company. He said he knew, but he would appreciate it if I would come anyway, and he wanted me to come that day. I had to rearrange my schedule, but, as I said, Jack is a hard man to say no to. When I arrived Jack was sitting at his desk, but he wasn't smiling. He was obviously very upset. When I asked him what was wrong, he took out a videotape and played it for me. He had been on another TV program, and the host nailed him to the wall, took him down off the wall, and nailed him back up again. Only the second time he did it upside down and made Jack look not only wrong but like a fool. It was no contest. Jack's training by a media expert hadn't done any good. He was obviously not ready for that kind of rough interview. After the tape, he started talking about his experience. He said that he wanted my honest opinion. He asked, had he done as badly as he thought, and I answered, yes, he had. He said he knew he had, but he wasn't quite sure why. In fact, he was shocked that he had cracked under pressure. He went on to tell me that he had been in combat and had been under a great deal of pressure many times in his life, and he had never cracked before. He said it was terrible that the first time he broke was in public. He referred to the reporter as that dirty blankity-blank and went on to say that even when dealing with that dirty blankity-blank he should have been able to do better. He was surprised that the reporter scored so many points.

The first thing I said was that I wasn't a TV expert, and that if he really wanted constructive criticism, he should have a television professional look at the interview. He said that he would, but insisted that I give him my opinion then and there. I told him the first thing that struck me is that there were two types of interviews. In the first type, where he did so well, the object of the program was entertainment, and the interviewer tried to draw information from him and to make the program as lively as possible. When he asked a question that seemed to be antagonistic, the only purpose was to elicit a reaction. He was not out to get

Jack, but the last reporter was, and justifiably so. Jack's company had made a decision with which many members of the public disagreed, and he was on the program to defend that decision. The reporter thought it was his duty, not simply to question his thinking on the subject, but to get at the truth. He decided the best way to do that was to attack Jack's position. And since the interviewer knew exactly what he was doing and had been doing it for years, and was a competent professional, my friend didn't stand a chance.

A Media Boot Camp

It wasn't really a dirty so-and-so versus the good guy. It was an expert versus an amateur, and the amateur came off looking like an amateur. Jack had been exposed to some of the tricks of television interviewers, but he had been exposed in a nonstress situation. The reason that he did so much better in Korea is that before the United States Army sent him into the high-stress situation of combat, they sent him through boot camp. And in boot camp they try to make the training as realistic as possible, and they certainly put him under pressure. He admitted that even with all this, when he first went into combat he was in a state of terror and was ineffective, and only after several months did he become an effective soldier. He admitted the only reason he lived long enough to become effective was that his commanding officer made sure that green troops were not asked to undertake the most difficult assignments. At that point I interrupted him. I said that obviously what he needed was a media boot camp. I suggested that, instead of going and taking those nice friendly lessons from that nice friendly young lady, he find someone to train him under more realistic conditions, which would include putting him under pressure during the mock interviews. I suggested further that in the future, if he decided to go on television to defend a controversial position taken by his company, he start with smaller programs, smaller audiences, and possibly less skillful interviewers, and that he build up his confidence and his expertise before attempting national television.

When I made the statement about media boot camp, he acted as if it already existed, and of course it didn't. But the idea lit a fire under him, and when I told him it didn't exist, he insisted that I form one to train the officers of his company. All I really did was gather some friends of mine together—a print reporter I'd worked with some years ago, another fellow I'd worked with in radio, and an old school buddy of mine who's a TV producer—and convinced them to work with Jack's executives. We sat down, the four of us, and drew up plans for a high-stress media school.

Our first decision was that everyone going through the program must have a very thorough physical, because we'd have to put them under physical as well as mental stress. We decided that the time that an executive or anyone else who deals with the media is likely to make a mistake is when he's tired or upset. Therefore we attempted to recreate similar pressures. Our entire purpose was to make the training as realistic as possible.

We took Jack and three of his top men out to my country place, and cut them off from the rest of the world for six days. We woke them at six o'clock in the morning, and the training started as soon as they got out of bed. In fact, while they were getting dressed and shaving, they were interviewed by the print reporter. He asked them a variety of questions, most of which were geared to trap them or to make them trip up in an important area. Then at breakfast he went over with each of them the mistakes they had made, and described the answer that would have served their purposes best. Throughout the rest of the day the print, TV, and radio reporters took turns interviewing each of the subjects. The interviews covered a wide range of topics, but we dealt mainly with potential trouble areas so that the training would be as realistic as possible. To make it difficult, we gave them first difficult, and then impossible positions to defend. The whole point of these exercises was to teach them a type of mental karate, to enable them to go up against reporters who had been practicing this mental karate all their lives. In addition, we attempted to put them under as much stress as possible. One day during the training, they were forced to stand for sixteen hours, and during that time they were interviewed, almost interrogated. Another day we interrogated them while they stood in their underwear. It was embarrassing, it was humiliating, but it was very effective. At the end of four days these very sophisticated executives were giving as good as they got, and they were doing it with consistency.

The effectiveness of our program proved itself several months later. Once again their company was faced with exactly the same problem. The president and two of the other executives were approached by the same reporters, only this time the stories came out, if not pro company, at least neutral. Without exception, those executives handled themselves beautifully. They did so because they understood what was going on, and because they had trained under pressure. As a result, when they were asked tough questions, they were able to handle them instead of going to pieces.

Since this worked so well, I immediately hired media people and started running a very exclusive high-pressure media boot camp for executives. Two years later I canceled the operation. The reason was simple: although top executives wanted to be trained, and told us that they really didn't mind being kicked around during training, they were not exactly telling the truth. We found that after we trained these executives they avoided us. They didn't want to meet or associate with the people who had seen them in demeaning or losing situations. As a result, we lost corporate clients. Since this was only a small part of my business, I decided it was better if I just dropped it. I believe someone out there who has a media background can create a very successful business running media boot camps for executives if he or she doesn't have to go back to the executives for other business.

Stress Training for Young Attorneys

Once our firm developed the techniques for training business people under stress, we used them in a whole variety of ways. A good example was with a law firm. I was brought in to teach the young associates how to dress when they were dealing with various types of judges and juries. In between the sessions I started talking to one of the other instructors, who was a partner in the firm. He said that the real problem these young attorneys had was not their clothing. It was that they were often rattled by tough judges, and that some judges took pleasure in putting young attorneys through the wringer. What he really wanted to see was a way to teach the young attorneys how to handle that problem, but he hadn't been able to find one. I then told him about my experience with corporate executives and the media, and said that if he could come up with a similar type of training for his young attorneys, it would probably help. A few days later he called me back and asked me to help design an attorneys' boot camp. After some discussion we decided that the partners in the firm would drill young attorneys in role-playing games. The partners played the parts of the judges and attempted to rattle the young attorneys in a variety of ways. They used some of the same techniques they'd seen judges use, and when they finished they critiqued how the attorneys had handled themselves. It was their equivalent of legal boot camp. They set up little confrontation periods at lunch, and during every lunch one senior partner would play the judge and one of the young associates would be put on the defensive. The young associates in the firm hated it. They found themselves embarrassed and frequently inadequately prepared. However, the partners said that after only a few short weeks of this training, the young attorneys were handling themselves far better in the courtrooms.

After having applied stress training in half a dozen situations, I reported the results of this training in a research letter that I distribute to my corporate clients. I stated that at the time I had no statistics on the validity of the research, but had some very positive results from a dozen training experiences, and suggested that my clients consider using stress training in their in-house programs. It was almost a footnote in the research letter and I didn't expect it to elicit much response, but I was wrong. The response was enormous and I was almost overwhelmed and spent the next year or so traveling throughout the country helping client firms set up stress training.

Sales Stress Training

The most popular stress training was sales training. One of the essential, and neglected, elements of sales training is the reaction of salespeople to stress. We found that salespeople, particularly poor ones, reacted to stress, and as a result often sent very strong negative signals when their products were attacked by vigorous or antagonistic customers. To help them handle this type of situation while role-playing, we feigned vicious attacks on their products and on them personally. We started by having the boss or another salesperson play the part of an obnoxious customer. Then we became more sophisticated. We found that, since there were many types of customers who raised many types of objections to different products, we had to develop a stress training to cover each type of objection. In short, we taught salespeople to answer objections under pressure. Here again, the results were dramatic. Some salespeople who had never been able to handle customers successfully, who had really been order takers, found themselves, for the first time, handling customers and taking control of rather difficult sales situations. As a result, their sales increased dramatically. We found the training was particularly effective for younger salespeople, especially those who had never sold before. It gave them an instant feel for sales, and an instant self-assurance, because they knew they could handle the toughest customer.

Public Speaking

We also use this type of pressure training to train public speakers. Our most successful client was the wife of a congressional candidate, a very pleasant, intelligent woman who was frightened to death of speaking to an audience. She had been to three different speech coaches and did well during training. But the minute she stood up before a real audience, she became nervous and stiff and her fear showed in her face; as a result, her campaigning for her husband was counterproductive, and she knew it. Because the candidate had worked for one of my corporate clients, he knew of my work and asked me if I could help his wife. I said I didn't know if I could, but I'd try. I explained to her that she cracked under pressure and that her only hope was to be retrained under pressure. When she showed up for our training session, we had fifty balloons with faces painted on them facing her, and half a dozen people in the audience. We let her speak the first two times without interference, and the second time she gave a beautiful presentation. However, the third time she gave a little five-minute speech, we started shifting chairs and making noises. This broke her up, but she finally got used to it. By the end of the second day, we were screaming obscenities, banging chairs, telling her her husband was a crook, and she was carrying on as if we weren't there. In fact, she got so good that she started answering our jibes. In less than one month, she was back on the campaign trail. Two months later she spoke to an audience that was anything but friendly. When they shouted obscenities, she ignored them and carried on. When I called to congratulate her, she said it wasn't necessary, they weren't half as nasty as my people, and handling them was a cinch. She wasn't facing a new situation. She was convinced she could handle a very rough audience, because she'd been trained to do so. I believe that if she had completed only a standard speaking course, she would have fallen apart under those circumstances, even if she had learned to handle a regular audience.

The Stress Interview

The most successful use of self-developed stress training I've seen has been by college students preparing for job interviews. I speak to college students all the time and one of their favorite subjects is how to handle a job interview. After I tell them what is expected, I recommend that they conduct stress interviews with each other, and that the person playing the part of the instructor treat the interviewee very roughly so that when he is in a real interview, stress will seem to be a normal part of it, and he will be prepared for it. College students are ingenious when it comes to creating stress. They become almost sadistic. One group of young women said they took turns sitting on a high stool in the middle of the room while one person interviewed them, and the other people in the background made fun of them, poked at them, screamed in their ears. The object of the exercise was to teach the participant to be perfectly poised, not to be rattled, no matter what happened, and to give off only positive signals, even when someone was insulting her hair, her dress, and her family. They said they played the game for almost six weeks before they went for interviews, and they reported that during real interviews the stress was almost unnoticeable because it was so much less than what they were used to. It was almost like lifting a fifty-pound weight and then lifting a twenty-pound weight, it seemed so easy. The system, of course, works for men as well as women. I have received hundreds of letters from college students who froze at one interview after another until they had several hours of stress interview training, and then handled the next interview with poise. Based on these letters alone, I suggest that anyone who has an important interview, which must create a certain amount of stress, get together with a few friends or with his or her spouse, and rehearse at least twenty stress mock interviews. In fact, if you're going to be put into any situation in which you're going to have to perform under pressure, you'll do better if you practice under pressure.

Since I'm suggesting that men practice interviewing with their wives and women with their husbands and college students with one another, obviously the person playing the part of the interviewer or stress producer is not going to be as threatening as the real-world person who creates stress—the boss, the potential customer, etc. You can overcome this problem by creating stress artificially. There are many ways to create stress, and we've found several that work particularly well. First, you can put people under psychological stress by putting them under physical stress. If you force the subject to interview while sitting in a chair that is not there, the physical strain of holding oneself in that position is enormous and will create psychological stress. Or you can scream at the other person. We found that volume produces stress. The only problem you might have is that the subject of the training can't shout back. The person who's practicing to sell, to interview, or to speak must conduct himself as he wishes to conduct himself in the real situation using the same tone of voice he intends to use there.

Distractions also cause stress. If you practice to speak or to interview while someone is pounding a drum behind you, or rattling your chair, or jumping up and down, or shining a light in your eyes, that will create an artificial stress. If you can learn to perform under those circumstances, you'll find it easier to do it in the real-life situation. Once you learn to perform an activity while experiencing one type of stress, it gives you the self-assurance to perform under a different type of stress, particularly if the second type of stress isn't as obvious as the first. If you can give a perfect sales presentation or a speech while someone is shouting in your ear, banging a drum, yelling at you, or waving flags in front of you, there is almost nothing an audience or an interviewer can do that will rattle you. Self-assurance comes with practice under pressure.

CHAPTER TEN

Interpreting Your Personal Productivity Chart

First Glance

After you've been keeping a personal productivity chart for a month or so, you'll be aware of many of your shortcomings, and you will probably have subconsciously started to readjust your work style to correct them. Even if you have not, once you've read through your personal productivity chart, problem areas and solutions will jump off the pages. Most of you will notice that there are certain times during the day when you seem to slow down, are prone to mistakes, and are easily distracted. In addition, you may also notice that you put too much of your time and effort into certain aspects of your work, and too little into others. As I said, when you become aware of flaws in your work patterns, your natural instinct will be to correct them immediately, but you're going to have to restrain yourself. We found that people increased their productivity much more quickly if they ran their personal productivity charts for the recommended time, and then planned their improvements instead of attempting to improve as they go. It is for this reason that we suggest that you read through all of your charts several times before you make any decision as to how, when, and where you want to improve.

After reviewing your personal productivity chart several times, most but not all of your shortcomings will jump off your page. During our training sessions we noticed that when workers interpreted their personal productivity charts after one or two readings, they usually identify the mistakes they were looking for, and skip those they weren't. This is easy to do because you'll be looking at twenty to thirty pages of detailed and sophisticated information. It would take an extraordinary person with an extraordinary memory and statistical sense to correlate all of the various aspects of a personal productivity chart, and do it effectively, without using a pencil and a paper. To aid you in doing this, we've developed a series of forms that will help you analyze your personal productivity chart.

Project Form

The first form is a project form (see pages 186–87). It has five headings: Project, Time, Grade, Deadline, Comment. Before you attempt to fill out this form, you must review all your personal productivity sheets and identify all major projects. Then list them on this form in the order of their importance. If you're an attorney, you'll probably list cases: Smith vs. Jones, the Molloy file, the X case, the Y case. If you're a salesperson, you might list the top clients or even new products, or both. If you're an engineer, you'll probably list those projects that ate up a substantial amount of your time. You'll notice we have room for only four projects. If you have undertaken more than four major projects in a month, or if the nature of your work demands that you list more, you're going to have to extend this project form on your own. No matter how many projects you think you've identified, I suggest that you list only six, because after that you'll be listing less important work. If all your projects take about the same amount of time, choose those that will or did have the greatest impact on your success, and/or on your ability to be productive.

In the second column, record the amount of time you've spent on each job. This means, once again, going back through your work-flow sheets and recording each unit of time spent on a job. Here you have to be very careful. Let's assume you're an attorney, you go to court on Monday, and while there you handle two cases. Part of the time spent handling these cases obviously is a trip to and from court. If you spend only 10 percent of your time in the courthouse on one case and 90 percent on the other, it would seem inappropriate to allow half of the travel time to each case. But if you had to show up in court for either case, it would also be inappropriate to list 90 percent for one and 10 percent for the other. You're going to have to make a value judgment on how much time is to be assigned to each case. You may already have this information on your earlier form. If you do, simply record it, but don't do it too quickly. Often when looking at personal productivity sheets several weeks after they've been completed, the preparers decide that they don't know how to describe a job because they didn't enter enough detailed information on the charts. If this is true in your case, you may have to stop at this point and redo some, if not all, of your personal productivity sheets. You can do some estimating when filling out these forms, but wild guessing is a waste of time.

In the third column we ask for grades. You will notice there are the same number of spaces in the third column that there are in the second. We would like you to put the grade opposite the amount of time you spend achieving that grade. This is critical for making an accurate evaluation of your work. If you take a look at the sample chart on page 186, you'll notice that I filled in 340 minutes in the ninth space, and that my grade was 94. Since the grade is well above average, it should have a greater effect on the final grade, because obviously it had a greater impact on the entire project. I don't insist that you do a strict mathematical analysis of time and grade to come up with a final grade, but I do suggest you weigh more heavily the grades given to key areas in the project—areas that are important because you spent more time on them or because you've made critical decisions while working on them. Obviously, if you have time slots without grades, you can leave them blank or you can estimate. The final grade, however, should be more than a product of mathematics. It requires that you make a decision. You may have spent thirteen major time units during the month on the Molloy case, and you may have given yourself 84 as an average each time. Now, at the end of the case, you decide it didn't really run very well and the entire case is only worth a 76. Obviously, the chart is much more accurate if the last grade is 76, but, since this is an estimate, we would like you to circle it so that in the future you will know it is an estimate.

The fourth column is headed Deadline. Here we would like you to note if you've missed any deadlines, either interim deadlines or final ones. You should record if there was a number of times when you worked late, rushed through any part of a project, or were affected with deadlineitis.

In the final column make comments about the job. You can re-record the comments you made earlier or add to them. While we invite all comments on this sheet, the ones that will help most are positive ones—comments that are really suggestions that will help you perform better in the future if you run across the same type of assignment.

Activity Form

Form II is the Activity Form. This page has only four columns. In the first you list the type of activity performed, in the second the time spent, in the third the time lost, and in the final one the grades you gave yourself for performing each activity.

As you can see by looking at the sample form (see page 188), by activity we mean the type of work done and not the job itself. For example, if you're an attorney, don't write down "Smith vs. Jones." Look at the Smith vs. Jones file and see how much time you spent in court and how much time you spent in doing preparation. If you spent one hour doing each, Smith vs. Jones would be recorded in two activity files, 60 minutes for clerical and 60 minutes for court work. As we pointed out earlier, it isn't important how you divide your work; what is essential is that you don't mix activities. If for one project you put everything under preparation, including your trip to the library, travel, working at the computer, and talking to three people about the job, you must not list each of these separately when you record your other projects. The only thing you must be absolutely certain about is that you are consistent, otherwise this form falls apart.

We found it works best if you fill in the second, third, and fourth columns at the same time. The time spent on a project is self-explanatory. If you spent from nine in the morning until ten working on a job, put down 60 minutes. It's easier if you list all the times in minutes, because obviously every job isn't going to break evenly into hours. Under Time Lost list the amount of time you were supposed to be working when you were not. If between nine and ten you only accomplished 30 minutes' worth of work, then you have 30 minutes in the Time Lost section. Notice on this form that the Time Lost and the Grade sections are identical except for the headings. The reason is the same as the reason we had identical columns in the last form: you'll find it easier to interpret these forms when you're finished if you make sure the boxes correspond to one another. One of the purposes of filling out these forms is to give you a visual grasp of information, and since this form lets you see everything at once, you can correlate it very easily. There are certain advantages of such a system. One of the most obvious is that if you have 60 minutes in box one and 30 minutes in box two, and you gave yourself a grade of 70, you'll understand immediately that you're being a very lenient marker. As with the earlier chart, you may not have grades for every element of your work. If you don't, you can assign a grade now and circle it, indicating that it's an estimate, or you can simply leave it blank. Remember that these forms are being filled out for your benefit, not someone else's, so the decision is strictly personal.

You must try to fill out these forms accurately, even if that's embarrassing. Almost all those who fill in the activity form are surprised at the amount of time they spend on certain aspects of their work. We found, for example, that many top executives operate best when dealing with complicated and complex matters, and that their performance is poorest when dealing with simple clerical details. The mistakes they make and the amount of time they waste while performing these seemingly simple clerical functions can often be embarrassing. Most of them, when they first look at the activity form, are astounded at the amount of time they spend doing things that their secretaries should be doing, and many of them, as a result of this form, decide to change their work style. The most common solution is to attack those aspects of their work that they find boring and at which their performance level is low, with as much intensity as possible. The idea is to improve performance through sheer effort. Of course, there are some who are in more fortunate positions. The president of one company, after looking at his chart, hired another secretary—with good reason. He said he was paid more than seventy dollars an hour and found he was spending one-third of his time doing the work of a secretary who earned less than ten dollars an hour.

If, after reading this chart, you don't decide to reorder your priorities and reorder your work schedule, you're indeed a rare individual. Over 90 percent of the people who completed the activity form changed their priorities, or at least their style of work, as a result of seeing in black and white what they'd been doing with their time. The misappropriation of time sometimes jumps off the form, and as a result this is one of the more valuable forms you can fill out.

Interruption Chart

The next form is the Interruption Chart (see page 189), which has three columns: Source, Time, Time Lost. The sources of interruptions are obvious. Go through your work-flow sheets and identify all those people, places, or things that are sources of interruption. Then, try to guess which one has interrupted you most often, and make that your primary source of interruption and list it in column one. You will note that columns two and three are identical in form and the reason is the same as the reason in the earlier forms: we wish you to correlate the information. You should also notice that there are exactly thirty spaces in each column. If you've filled in the chart for the recommended six weeks, this will give you one space for each day for each source of interruption. It will also enable you to identify exactly how many times during the first day, second day, and third day you were interrupted by any one source, and the amount of time lost to that source. This will give you a very clear picture of how your time is being wasted by any person, place, or thing. You will note that at the bottom of this form there is a place for you to record what steps you intend to take to correct any problems that are pointed out by the form. Please fill in this section of the chart as soon as you finish. We found, working with students and businesspeople, that when they committed to improvements in writing, they were twice as likely to carry out those improvements efficiently and immediately.

Work Calendar

The next form is the Work Calendar (see page 190). We developed this form so that you can see at a glance if there are any times during the week when you're unproductive or very productive. Filling in this form is simple. There are six spaces in each block, and each block covers one hour of one day of the week. In the first space you fill in the number of minutes you lost between eight and nine on Monday of the first week. In the second slot you fill in the time you lost between eight and nine on Monday of the second week, the same for Monday of the third week, and so on. Then, in the final slot, you add all of those times together. Obviously, you're going to have to fill in the same information for the rest of Monday, nine to ten, ten to eleven, and so on, and then progress to Tuesday, Wednesday, Thursday, and Friday. Obviously, too, if you work nights or you work a six-day week, you're going to have to develop your own chart or rework this one, but the result will be the same.

Most of those who have been through the program found this form useful. Almost all of those filling in the chart identified certain times during the day, and days during the week, when there were predictable letdowns in their productivity. In addition, most of them recognized that there were times during the day and during the week when interruptions in their work were more damaging than others. You may find if you're interrupted at ten in the morning you go back to work immediately, but if you're interrupted at two or three in the afternoon the interruption has a far greater impact, because by that time your mind is ready to drift out the window. Those who have faced this problem said that they overcame it by making sure they weren't interrupted during those low points, and by planning their days and their weeks so that they didn't undertake vital or critical tasks during their low points.

Several very successful executives now avoid making important decisions or holding meetings or working on important projects during their low periods. In addition, we found that if you structure your work very carefully during these periods, you can maintain a high level of productivity, particularly if the work is not that demanding.

Please remember when dealing with these forms that solutions don't have to be complicated. You don't have to restructure your whole life or even your work life. In fact, the simplest solution is usually the best one, and if anything occurs to you immediately, try it. There were dozens and dozens of people who recognized that their blood-sugar level went down at two or three in the afternoon, and a coffee break at that time was more productive than unproductive. There were also people who said they couldn't get started before eleven o'clock, and set up schedules for themselves the night before so that they would be sure to be busy between nine and eleven—or, as one executive put it, "until his natural juices got flowing." What this form uncovers is your individual clock, and almost everyone has one. When these calendars helped uncover serious flaws in productivity, we found that different students used different approaches to correct them. Some simply changed their clock. They were able to affect the way they worked, and when they worked best. Others adjusted to their clock. They looked upon their clock as biological and unchangeable, and made realistic adjustments in their work to suit it. There were some who did both. They usually made the most progress, because they recognized they had a clock and they adjusted their work to it without letting this internal clock dominate their work style.

Please remember that these forms are not written in stone. They're not absolutes. They've been developed over a period of years by people much like you attempting to improve their productivity. Therefore, if you find a form that does not work for you, change it or skip it. It isn't going to destroy your productivity training, but please don't rationalize yourself into not filling out these forms. If you can fill out one, do it, because most of these forms work for most people. Remember, the whole point of these forms is to commit your daily activities and your plans for improvement to writing. Both students and top executives admitted that, after they did, they did less fuzzy thinking and procrastinating.

Debriefing Form

These were not the only forms our students tried. There are a number of forms that were developed by individuals that worked for them, but wouldn't work for everyone. For example, three men and two women in our program developed debriefing forms. Two were in sales, two were attorneys, and one was an executive in an engineering firm. All five developed their own unique forms. Each decided independently that the best type of analysis was an instant review, and that debriefing worked only for certain activities—activities that are almost impossible to put on a personal productivity chart. An obvious example was given by one of our attorneys. He said that he couldn't run a work-flow chart on how well he was doing while defending a client in court. We had similar comments from pilots about landing planes, and other men and women who make critical decisions in public—politicians, salespeople, actors, etc. The two attorneys who decided to do postmortems on their courtroom work went about it as follows: as soon as they left the court, they sat down and attempted to analyze in writing what they'd done and to decide what changes they would make, either on the next day or on the next occasion they faced a similar situation. The attorneys volunteered to do this because it was one of the procedures recommended in law school. We found a great deal of difficulty talking salespeople into adopting the same procedure after a major sales presentation, and yet for them it was more critical, since invariably they sell the same products to the same types of people over and over. While almost one hundred people ran debriefing on critical activities, it didn't succeed with everyone, but was useful only in about 60 percent of the cases. It generally worked for those engaged in activities that required performance under pressure—public speakers, attorneys, salespeople, executives, etc.

I describe these debriefing forms not because everyone needs one, but because I think you should consider developing one for your activities if you think it's appropriate, and to tell you that you can make up this form or any other form that you think is necessary. You don't have to rely on the forms you find in this book. Many of our students developed individual forms that worked only for them. They were tailored to a particular situation or even a unique job, and in most cases they worked very well. The fact is that there are so many activities in the work world that there is no form or set of forms that will work for everyone. If you decide that the personal productivity chart or any other form does not adequately measure what you do, feel free to change it to suit your needs or to create a new form.

Since the forms have a double function—first, to help you see exactly what you're doing, and, second, to help you to improve—we're going to ask you to go back through your work-flow chart and identify your three most typical days. Pick out three days in which your performance was not its best and not its worst, but average. Choose days on which you performed tasks that you are likely to repeat in the future. If you only travel four days a year, don't choose a day when you were on the road. If you are an attorney and you spend 80 percent of your time in a courtroom, don't pick a day when you did only library work. If you're an attorney who only goes to court twice a year, don't pick those days when you were in court. Pick days that are typical in every way. Try not to pick three days in the same week. It's better if the chosen days come from three different weeks, but it's more important that they be typical than evenly spread.

Take these and enter them in the personal productivity charts one, two, and three (see pages 191–93). Leave personal productivity charts four through thirteen (pages 194–97) blank for the present. You're going to use them in the future, because part of your training is to run a one-week personal productivity chart after six months, a year, two years, and three years. On charts four, five, six, and seven, you'll take the most typical day from each of those weeks, and record it as a permanent record. By putting days from different personal productivity charts next to the original personal productivity chart, you'll be able to see in which areas you've improved, and in which areas improvement is still needed. You'll be able to evaluate your progress, see if there's been any slipping, and retrain yourself when needed.

Steps for Immediate Improvement

Although there is no definite method of correcting your flaws, there is a general pattern that most of our successful students followed.

Most found it easiest to start by rearranging their physical environment. If your desk is facing out the window, as mine was, and you find by putting it against the wall you can work more effectively, take that first and most obvious step. If you need better lighting, arrange to get it. If your chair is too comfortable, or not comfortable enough, trade it in for a better one.

Second, arrange to handle the people in your life more effectively. If your secretary interrupts you all the time, see that she stops. If you have lunch with someone who has a liquid lunch and it makes you ineffective for the rest of the day, either avoid having lunch with that person, or make it a point not to drink as much at lunch.

Third, rearrange your work schedule. I suggest before you do this that you read the chapter on organization.

Fourth, identify times during your workday when you will be engaged in specific activities and when you will not allow yourself to be interrupted. This will allow you to avoid those interruptions that critically impair your ability to be productive.

Fifth, look at your work flow and decide whether you're putting too much emphasis on certain types of work, and rearrange your priorities. If you're spending four-fifths of your time on clients who produce 20 percent of your profit, as is the case with many salespeople, you have to rearrange your schedule.

Sixth and last, look at yourself realistically, and appraise your ability to work. Identify your strong and weak points. Decide exactly where you need improvement most, and where you want to improve first. Take definite steps toward that improvement. Set up a game plan. Develop goals. Draw up a calendar of improvement, then start today.

FORM I
PROJECT FORM

Project 1	Time			Grade			Deadline	Comment
Molloy	40	30	26	90	70	90	Missed	
	7	28	14	80	80	71	159 deadline	1) Should have planned better
	16	109	340	72	86	94		
	104	16	05	98	80	80	Made up	
	16	__	__	90	__	__	Time	
	__	__	__	__	__	__	On schedule	2) Should have done more work at home
	__	__	__	__	__	__		
	__	__	__	__	__	__		More should have been done by assistant
	TOTAL ___			AVERAGE	84	76		3) Poor project
								4) Margin bid too low

Suggestions
How to Improve   1. _____   2. _____   3. _____

Project 2	Time			Grade			Deadline	Comment
	__	__	__	__	__	__		
	__	__	__	__	__	__		
	__	__	__	__	__	__		
	__	__	__	__	__	__		
	__	__	__	__	__	__		
	__	__	__	__	__	__		
	__	__	__	__	__	__		
	__	__	__	__	__	__		
	TOTAL ___			AVERAGE ___				

Suggestions
How to Improve   1. _____   2. _____   3. _____

PROJECT FORM
(cont'd)

Project 3	Time	Grade	Deadline	Comment
	— — —	— — —		
	— — —	— — —		
	— — —	— — —		
	— — —	— — —		
	— — —	— — —		
	— — —	— — —		
	— — —	— — —		
	— — —	— — —		
	TOTAL _____	AVERAGE _____		

Suggestions
How to Im-
prove   1. _____ 2. _____ 3. _____

Project 4	Time	Grade	Deadline	Comment
	— — —	— — —		
	— — —	— — —		
	— — —	— — —		
	— — —	— — —		
	— — —	— — —		
	— — —	— — —		
	— — —	— — —		
	— — —	— — —		
	TOTAL _____	AVERAGE _____		

Suggestions
How to Im-
prove   1. _____ 2. _____ 3. _____

Form II
Activity Form

Activity	Time	Time Lost	Grade
1) Clerical	—— —— ——	—— —— ——	—— —— ——
	—— —— ——	—— —— ——	—— —— ——
	—— —— ——	—— —— ——	—— —— ——
	—— —— ——	—— —— ——	—— —— ——
	—— —— ——	—— —— ——	—— —— ——
	—— —— ——	—— —— ——	—— —— ——
	—— —— ——	—— —— ——	—— —— ——
	—— —— ——	—— —— ——	—— —— ——
	—— —— ——	—— —— ——	—— —— ——
	—— —— ——	—— —— ——	—— —— ——
	—— —— ——	—— —— ——	—— —— ——
	TOTAL _____	TOTAL _____	FINAL _____
Steps to Improve **2)** Field Work	1. _____	2. _____	3. _____
	—— —— ——	—— —— ——	—— —— ——
	—— —— ——	—— —— ——	—— —— ——
	—— —— ——	—— —— ——	—— —— ——
	—— —— ——	—— —— ——	—— —— ——
	—— —— ——	—— —— ——	—— —— ——
	—— —— ——	—— —— ——	—— —— ——
	—— —— ——	—— —— ——	—— —— ——
	—— —— ——	—— —— ——	—— —— ——
	TOTAL _____	TOTAL _____	FINAL _____
Steps to Improve	1. _____	2. _____	3. _____

INTERRUPTION CHART

Source	Time	Time Lost
	—— —— ——	—— —— ——
	—— —— ——	—— —— ——
	—— —— ——	—— —— ——
	—— —— ——	—— —— ——
	—— —— ——	—— —— ——
	—— —— ——	—— —— ——
	—— —— ——	—— —— ——
	—— —— ——	—— —— ——
	—— —— ——	—— —— ——
	—— —— ——	—— —— ——
	TOTAL ———	TOTAL ———
Corrective Steps	1. ———————	2. ———————
	—— —— ——	—— —— ——
	—— —— ——	—— —— ——
	—— —— ——	—— —— ——
	—— —— ——	—— —— ——
	—— —— ——	—— —— ——
	—— —— ——	—— —— ——
	—— —— ——	—— —— ——
	—— —— ——	—— —— ——
	TOTAL ———	TOTAL ———
Corrective Steps	1. ———————	2. ———————

Work Calendar

TIME	Monday	Tuesday	Wednesday	Thursday	Friday
8.	—— TOTAL ——	—— TOTAL ——	—— TOTAL ——	—— TOTAL ——	—— TOTAL ——
9.	—— TOTAL ——	—— TOTAL ——	—— TOTAL ——	—— TOTAL ——	—— TOTAL ——
10.	—— TOTAL ——	—— TOTAL ——	—— TOTAL ——	—— TOTAL ——	—— TOTAL ——
11.	—— TOTAL ——	—— TOTAL ——	—— TOTAL ——	—— TOTAL ——	—— TOTAL ——
12.	—— TOTAL ——	—— TOTAL ——	—— TOTAL ——	—— TOTAL ——	—— TOTAL ——
1.	—— TOTAL ——	—— TOTAL ——	—— TOTAL ——	—— TOTAL ——	—— TOTAL ——
2.	—— TOTAL ——	—— TOTAL ——	—— TOTAL ——	—— TOTAL ——	—— TOTAL ——
3.	—— TOTAL ——	—— TOTAL ——	—— TOTAL ——	—— TOTAL ——	—— TOTAL ——
4.	—— TOTAL ——	—— TOTAL ——	—— TOTAL ——	—— TOTAL ——	—— TOTAL ——
5.	—— TOTAL ——	—— TOTAL ——	—— TOTAL ——	—— TOTAL ——	—— TOTAL ——
6.	—— TOTAL ——	—— TOTAL ——	—— TOTAL ——	—— TOTAL ——	—— TOTAL ——

JOHN T. MOLLOY'S
PERSONAL PRODUCTIVITY
CHART

Job	Time	Source of Interruption	Time Wasted	% My Fault	Additional Time Wasted	Comments, Quality & Quantity Score

John T. Molloy's
Personal Productivity
Chart

Job	Time	Source of Interruption	Time Wasted	% My Fault	Additional Time Wasted	Comments, Quality & Quantity Score

JOHN T. MOLLOY'S
PERSONAL PRODUCTIVITY
CHART

Job	Time	Source of Interruption	Time Wasted	% My Fault	Additional Time Wasted	Comments, Quality & Quantity Score

John T. Molloy's
Personal Productivity
Chart

Job	Time	Source of Interruption	Time Wasted	% My Fault	Additional Time Wasted	Comments, Quality & Quantity Score

JOHN T. MOLLOY'S
PERSONAL PRODUCTIVITY
CHART

Job	Time	Source of Interruption	Time Wasted	% My Fault	Additional Time Wasted	Comments, Quality & Quantity Score

JOHN T. MOLLOY'S
PERSONAL PRODUCTIVITY
CHART

Job	Time	Source of Interruption	Time Wasted	% My Fault	Additional Time Wasted	Comments, Quality & Quantity Score

JOHN T. MOLLOY'S
PERSONAL PRODUCTIVITY
CHART

Job	Time	Source of Interruption	Time Wasted	% My Fault	Additional Time Wasted	Comments, Quality & Quantity Score

JOHN T. MOLLOY'S
PERSONAL PRODUCTIVITY
CHART

Job	Time	Source of Interruption	Time Wasted	% My Fault	Additional Time Wasted	Comments, Quality & Quantity Score

JOHN T. MOLLOY'S
PERSONAL PRODUCTIVITY
CHART

Job	Time	Source of Interruption	Time Wasted	% My Fault	Additional Time Wasted	Comments, Quality & Quantity Score

John T. Molloy's
Personal Productivity
Chart

Job	Time	Source of Interruption	Time Wasted	% My Fault	Additional Time Wasted	Comments, Quality & Quantity Score

JOHN T. MOLLOY'S
PERSONAL PRODUCTIVITY
CHART

Job	Time	Source of Interruption	Time Wasted	% My Fault	Additional Time Wasted	Comments, Quality & Quantity Score

JOHN T. MOLLOY'S
PERSONAL PRODUCTIVITY
CHART

Job	Time	Source of Interruption	Time Wasted	% My Fault	Additional Time Wasted	Comments, Quality & Quantity Score

JOHN T. MOLLOY'S
PERSONAL PRODUCTIVITY
CHART

Job	Time	Source of Interruption	Time Wasted	% My Fault	Additional Time Wasted	Comments, Quality & Quantity Score

Index

ABOUT THE AUTHOR

JOHN T. MOLLOY is the author of *Live for Success* and two earlier books—*Dress for Success* and *The Woman's Dress for Success* —which have sold over two and a half million copies and have literally changed the look of corporate America.

These books, along with Molloy's research techniques, are taught in hundreds of universities both in the U.S. and abroad. He has also been a consultant to over 380 of the Fortune 500 companies, to scores of the largest companies in Europe and Japan, and to dozens of governments.

A lecturer in wide demand, Molloy speaks frequently before corporate and university groups. In addition, he is a contributing editor to *Success* magazine, author of a nationally syndicated newspaper column, and host of a weekly talk show on ABC network radio.